The Ultimate Learning Experience

*A young man's journey
through the choices of life.*

CHRIS SKINNER

The Chris Skinner Organizations, Inc.
P. O. Box 1558
Radford, VA 24143-1558

This book is dedicated in loving memory
of my Aunt Janice Faye Wells
(1963–1980)

Contents

Acknowledgements

I would like to acknowledge Natalie Atkins, my editor, for her suggestions, corrections, and insights. Thank you for your expertise.

I would like to acknowledge Gary and Jackie Smith of Wells-Smith Partners, my uncle and aunt, for the cover design. It is more than I could have asked for. Thank you for your love and support.

I would like to acknowledge Taunya Waxham, Artzy-One Studio Design & Illustration for design and technical production assistance in getting this book into print. I could not have accomplished it without your help.

I would like to acknowledge Susan Kwilecki, Ph.D. for her support, encouragement, and advice during my undergraduate studies and beyond. Thank you for always being my teacher.

I would like to acknowledge the doctors, nurses, physical therapists, occupational therapists, radiologists, surgeons and all the medical personnel who used their knowledge to save my life. Thank you for doing your job so well.

I would like to acknowledge all the many friends, both old and new, who helped me through my ultimate learning experience. Your assistance in the hospital, at rehab centers, and when I returned to school was vital to my success. Thank you for being there. I don't want to miss any names. These are the people who gave their time to help me through this: Trisha Amstutz, Sarah Anderson, Jennifer Ashby, Brandi Barnes, Kate

Acknowledgements

Baxter, Emilee Baber, Kate Biglin, Holly Bush, Anne Brie, Jaime Cassavechia, Jason Coleman, Kyle Cousins, Melissa Cumbie, Rhea Drake, The Ells family, Meghan Farrell, Whitney Funk, Shane Guynn, Jaime Harper, Kelly Hicks, Kim Johnson, Devin Kizer, Amy & Josh Kuerentjes, Daniel Lee, Amber Maggard, Maureen McCarthy, Reagan McGuire, Rachel McKinley, Tiffany Miller, Kimberly Morehead, Megan Pitcock, Vanessa White, Fritz Schindler, Tracy Shulsinger, Annie Smith, Crystal Tucker, Kandi Turner, Natalie Vines, Maureen Weyer, Maureen Wiedel, Brenda Willner, Paul Wodjwla, Coleman Winstead. There are so many more of you and you know who you are. Thank you all!

I would like to acknowledge Josh Chiprut, my roommate for his unfailing friendship. We began this journey together and I am so thankful that we finished together.

I would like to acknowledge my friend, Stephen Bailey. Once we were fraternity brothers and today we are brothers in Christ. Thank you for your belief in my mission to save lives and your decision to be a part of it.

I would like to acknowledge Robin Clark, my mentor. Your pep talks, words of wisdom, and perspective on life were invaluable to keep me focused. I will always cherish our friendship.

I would like to acknowledge Pastor Rich Palmer and his wife Debbie Palmer for their love and support. You taught me so much about life and about God. Thank you for the time you spent with me.

I would like to acknowledge my grandfather and grandmother, Henry and Marcy Wells (Pepaw and Memaw) for their love and support. Thank you for the phone calls and the love you show to me, and all your children, grandchildren, and great-grandchildren every day of your life.

I would like to acknowledge my uncle, Steve Wells. Thank you for your love and faith in me when I didn't deserve it. My donkey finally crossed the finish line.

I would like to acknowledge my sister, Tamra Lanham for her love and support. Thank you for forgiving me for all the things in the past and standing by me in this time of need. I would not have made it at Radford without your help that first semester back.

I would like to acknowledge my brother, Patrick Skinner for his love and support. Thank you for changing your course to share a vision with me. Together we will make a difference.

I would like to acknowledge my father, Wayne Skinner. Thank you for standing by me and loving me. I believe this journey brought us together in a way that we never knew before.

I would like to acknowledge my stepfather, Michael Hinson for his unbelievable strength and support through this whole experience. Thank you for your love and for standing by my mother and me. Also, thank you for the great photos that were included in this book.

I would like to acknowledge my mother, Jeanne Hinson, for her love and dedication. You unselfishly gave everything you had to help me through this experience. You stood by me, took care of me, and loved me. You moved mountains and stood firm as my shield and protector. Thank you mother. You are amazing.

I would like to acknowledge my wife, Suzanne Jefferis Skinner. Without this experience, I would not have met the woman of my dreams. I thank you for your love and the joy you have brought into my life. I look forward to sharing my love and my life with you.

Acknowledgements

I must acknowledge my Lord and Savior, Jesus Christ who has held me in the palm of His hands through this entire experience. Thank You for Your unconditional love. Help me to always be humble and acknowledge Your path for my life.

Foreword

As a professor of Religious Studies at Radford University, it has been my privilege to know Chris Skinner since January 2001. Having drawn wisdom and hope from his "ultimate learning experience," I am delighted to introduce this autobiographical account of it.

At the University, I have a justified reputation as one of the most difficult and uncompromising instructors. My teaching philosophy exactly corresponds to the life approach Chris advises in the pages that follow. Students must demonstrate the self-discipline, perseverance, and accountability necessary for success in the Real World. Many drop or fail my classes.

Chris enrolled in "World Religions" the first semester he returned to school after his accident. Given his severe physical limitations, I seriously doubted he could meet my rigorous academic standards, even with disability accommodations. Still, his determination to try amazed me. In his place, I remember thinking, I would simply give up. As the semester progressed, he faced every imaginable difficulty—hospitalization for infections, dizziness and nausea that impaired concentration, wheelchair malfunctions, etc. The hurtful interaction with the empty-headed "cute blonde girl" (described in the chapter "My Return to RU") occurred in my class. Fortunately, I never learned her name.

Given all he had to contend with, I worried that Chris would fail the course, a discouragement I wanted no part in. Frankly, as I began reading him the first exam, I felt tempted to give facial or vocal hints. At the same time, I knew Chris to be too bright and honest to want high marks he had not earned. Better judgment prevailed; I put on my poker face and spoke in a monotone. By the fourth or fifth question, my anxiety disappeared—Chris needed no help from me to answer correctly. On an exam that plunged many of his "enabled" classmates irretrievably underwater, he scored a "B." Chris not only finished "World Religions" with that grade, but another course that included writing assignments. Completing two of my classes with a "B" makes him the academic equivalent of a Green Beret.

Chris' "ultimate learning experience" is a youthful, but no less profound, confrontation with timeless and universal truths—insights into life that, it so happens, correspond to venerable religious teachings. What did he learn? First, that we are all at the mercy of an unfathomable force—fate or chance—that can, at a moment's notice, transform ordinary life into an endless waking nightmare. He was not immune, Chris found out, and he accurately warns that no one is.

Chris' second realization is the hallmark of maturity: Appearances are deceptive, and we must always look deeper. Before the accident, Chris possessed what many people, young and old, crave—physical attractiveness, athletic ability, popularity, a schedule of pleasurable self-indulgence. Suddenly falling out of the in-crowd, as he did, taught not only the hidden dangers of this lifestyle, but also the fleeting nature of its satisfactions. All that glitters is not gold. Vice versa, disasters, Chris learned, can be opportunities for enduring achievement. In sum, there are higher and better aspirations than, in his words, "temporary fun."

This brings us to the third lesson, which Chris teaches by consummate example—the possibility of heroism. Heroes are people who respond to the worst conditions with the best qualities. It is difficult to imagine anything more devastating than Chris' accident and its aftermath, herein presented in un-flinching detail. Unsurprisingly, victims of such adversity often bitterly withdraw from life. It is nothing short of miraculous that Chris emerged championing, as he puts it, the "virtues" of "desire, determination, willpower, ambition, and persever-ance." While Chris is extraordinary, he reminds us that we all have heroic potential. As the sun daily rises, each of us not only can, but also must, choose between strength and weakness, self-discipline and self-indulgence, hanging on and giving up. Fate may dictate less than optimal circumstances, but, finally, we determine whether we become an asset or a liability to oth-ers and ourselves.

In the pages that follow, the reader will find a spectacular case of the triumph of light over darkness, a victory that is never easy or assured, but which ultimately rests in our own hands. I can think of no one more worthy of emulation by young and old alike than Chris Skinner.

Susan Kwilecki, Ph.D.
Professor of Religious Studies
Radford University

Introduction

My name is Chris Skinner and I have a disability. No, it isn't the obvious one you see as I roll around in my power wheelchair looking like half-man, half-car. I am paralyzed and do not have any feeling in my body from about the top of my chest down. I have to ask people to assist me with the most basic tasks that you may take for granted on a daily basis. I need assistance to eat meals, take showers, go to the bathroom, shave myself, brush my teeth, get in and out of my wheelchair, in and out of bed, put my clothes on, take my clothes off, open most doors, and much more. Believe it or not this is not the disability that I am speaking of. No, in fact the disability I am talking about is one that many people possess. Oh yes, you too may have this disability, wheelchair or no wheelchair. You may not have thought about it, or even be aware that it is classified as a disability. Scary thought?

I know what you're thinking, "I don't have a disability, you crazy man!" Well, just bear with me for a few moments, read on, and then decide whether or not I'm on point or off the wall. I can promise you that if you allow yourself to be honest about situations in your life, you will benefit from what I have to say.

This disability I refer to has been with me for as long as I can remember. I have to learn things the hard way. I've always been hardheaded about making decisions…and still am! It's not that I don't believe people when they tell me things, because I do—or at least I think I do. It's just that I choose to live my life to the fullest, and that sometimes means that I get caught up in the "living" and forget all about the consequences. So when my family, friends, teachers, ministers, scout leaders, coaches, or basically anyone for that matter told me of things to avoid, I often experienced them anyway.

Now be honest, does this sounds familiar to you? At least some of you are saying, "Oh yeah, that's me too." You see, we all have free will and as we get older that means we have the ability to do what we want and say what we feel. In essence, I'm talking about making decisions.

Since my accident I have had time to sit, be still, and evaluate my life and the environment around me. I consider this a luxury that most adults do not have time for, or maybe just don't take the time for. Think about it, when is the last time you have just sat in absolute silence and analyzed your life and observed your surroundings? You really should try it. You would be absolutely amazed with what you will learn about yourself and your life.

After spending several months on my back just staring at the ceiling, I came to the conclusion that I have had a disability all along. I would like to share with you little portions of my life that taught me valuable lessons that I learned while growing up and still continue to learn with every breath I take. I want more than anything for you to realize how important each and every decision you make in your everyday lives really is and consider the ultimate magnitude and lasting impact that the simplest decisions can have on your lives. I realize that we can't possibly make all the right decisions all the time, day in and day out. If we were able to do that then our lives would be perfect, wouldn't they? We all know that is not possible. However, I am saying if we could just consider our steps a little more wisely, it sure would make living a lot easier. I mean, come on think about it. Do you not agree?

My friends, (yes, I consider you a friend if you are reading this book) what I'm telling you is just plain common sense. We know that our lives will not run smoothly all the time and there will be times, like it or not, when we will be forced to deal with unpleasant consequences. We know this; in fact, we know it is inevitable. Now the question is, "How will you deal with the consequences?"

I can't force you to deal with consequences you may encounter in your life in a positive manner; in fact, no one can. However, I can assure you, my friends, that the only thing that can stop you from accomplishing your dreams is yourself. Do not let anyone negative keep you from success and happiness. Mark Twain says it best, "Keep away from people who try to belittle your ambitions. Small people always do that, but the really great make you feel that you, too, can become great."

Your future is in your hands. What I mean by that is with the right attitude, ambitions, goals, and desire to succeed the sky is the limit. In this book, I will narrate you through my personal experiences and share with you how I dealt with tragic circumstances and negative people. I can't begin to tell you how many times I have heard the words, "You can't do that," or "You are setting yourself up for failure." Or my very favorite, "You are being too aggressive and setting your goals too high." In spite of negative people, huge obstacles, and personal tragedy, I have overcome and persevered…and so can you.

I have a disability that can be seen by the naked eye, but you will realize as you read about my life that the real disability I possess lies deep inside. Coming face to face with disabilities, accepting them, and battling to conquer them I admit is the hardest thing I have ever done. Especially in my particular case, each day when I look in the mirror, I will always be reminded of a few decisions I made one summer night that lead to the irreversible consequence of being paralyzed. My goal is to encourage you to open your mind to think about your own life and the decisions you have made that could have impacted your life adversely. You may have never actually sat and thought deeply about this. Even if you have, do it some more. I can assure you this will help you learn more about yourself and grow as a person.

My hope, as you read this book, is that you realize just how fortunate you are and how precious your life really is. By taking this journey with me through my ultimate learning experience, I want you to gain a new appreciation for the value of the decisions you make every day. This very tragic accident was one of those defining moments in my life and as a result, I gained a new perspective. After months of rehab and soul-searching, I became determined that I would not give up. I want you to be able to put your own challenges into perspective and walk away with the knowledge that you can achieve your most desired goals. Instead of a tragic accident like mine, I want your defining moment to be the day you met Chris Skinner.

Chapter 1

In The Beginning

I came into this world kicking, screaming, and gasping for air on November 14, 1979 at Prince William Hospital in Manassas, Virginia. Jeanne Wells Skinner, my mother, was a full-time homemaker and stayed at home to be with my older brother Patrick and me. My father, Wayne Skinner, was a sales representative for a New York manufacturing company. He traveled quite a bit. We lived in a small, rural community about an hour outside of the Washington, D.C. metro area.

I was born during football season. The nursery staff randomly put NFL beanie hats on all the babies' heads. Mine was a Washington Redskins beanie, which I believe branded me a Redskins fan for life. I was the long awaited second child, and eventually became the middle child. When I was only two years old, my sister, Tammy, was born.

Fortunately, I was blessed with an outgoing personality, the smile of an angel (or devil, depending on your point of view), natural athletic abilities, and the determination of a bull. I have never been the kind of person who could be satisfied with just watching anything for very long. I needed physical activity, and lots of it. As a small child, I learned to walk by the time I was eight months old and I was riding a big wheel down steep hills by the time I was just twelve months old. A regular two-wheel bike came when I was just three years old. My parents were patient and believed that physically active children who were allowed to explore their worlds were more likely to have a successful life. Boy, were they in for a challenge!

I learned a great deal from my parents. They made sure we balanced our physical activity with mental activity. They taught me to read and do simple math problems by the time I was three years old. We read books and worked puzzles and built things with Legos daily. Other inside activities, as I grew older, included ping-pong, billiards, board games, card games, and projects on the computer.

We stayed outside a large part of each day, chasing grasshoppers, riding bikes, playing ball, planting gardens and taking walks. My parents spent endless hours playing basketball, baseball and tennis and riding bikes with me, my brother, and my sister. They didn't have to win like some of the parents of my friends always did. Instead, they challenged us to be winners by teaching us how to analyze the situation and make our own decisions.

Life was good for the Skinner siblings. However, my parents were having problems. It wasn't obvious to the three of us because of my father's work schedule, and because they worked hard to cover up any signs of discord. When we finally became aware that things were getting bad, we were devastated. We knew kids whose parents were divorced, and we didn't want to become a statistic like them. Our parents went to counseling and tried to make it work, but eventually were divorced.

We lived with my mother in a rental house on the Outer Banks of North Carolina. She worked as an accountant for a homebuilder and wasn't able to take very much time off. We did spend some time with our father, but the large part of our time was spent with our friends. Eventually, we fell into a comfortable routine. We often went to the beach together, after work and school, and on most weekends. My sister excelled in dance classes. My brother and I continued to be involved in sports activities, like surfing, basketball, soccer and baseball.

I played tennis with my mother almost everyday. She patiently hit shots to my forehand and backhand, carefully placing them to strengthen my abilities. Amazingly, I usually won the match, but each game was close and challenging. I'm sure at first she could have beaten the pants off me, but what would that have accomplished? I might have become frustrated and quit playing. Instead, she taught me the game and taught me to meet challenges at the same time. She eventually turned me over to the tennis pro to continue my lessons, but didn't end our practice sessions. That's how I learned each sport, except golf, and I wanted to play them all. I could watch a sport on TV for about ten minutes before I had to go out and play it myself. I was not a couch potato.

My mother met my stepfather, Mike Hinson, through their mutual friends. They began dating and were married a little over a year later. We moved to Franklin, Virginia, a mill town just outside of the Hampton Roads area when I was fourteen. My stepfather was the plant manager of the sawmill. The move was a mixed bag of blessings for me. In a school of less than seven hundred students, I easily made a name for myself by joining various clubs and playing on all the high school sports teams.

It was a small town, especially for a teenager; my friends and I had nothing to do in our spare time besides looking for places to hang out and drinking beer. Gone were the days of surfing and lying out on the beach. Fortunately, I was involved in so many positive activities that there was little time for anything else. My mother and stepfather encouraged and supported my interest in sports.

From the time I was four years old, I played some form of organized sports. I was always selected for the all-stars teams and was considered one of the better players. I was the junior tennis champion on the Outer Banks until we moved away. In high school, I played varsity golf, varsity basketball, varsity baseball, and varsity wrestling. I always had at least one sport to play that completely obsessed me…for a season. When the season ended, I moved on to the next one at hand. My coaches told me that I could play in college, if I would concentrate on just one sport year round. They were probably right. I just didn't see my chances until it was too late.

When I decided to learn to play golf, it was because I needed a fall sport to play and I didn't want to play football. I was one of the fastest kids in the school and the football coaches were after me to come out for football. Sure I was fast, but I wasn't big enough to play football. So I asked my mother for a junior membership to the country club and a set of used golf clubs. Taking this as a learning experience, she agreed on the basis of a contract between us. She would pay for the junior membership at the club and $100 for the used golf clubs, if I would keep my hair cut short the way she liked it. My brother was off at college and was wearing his hair shoulder length and she hated it. I agreed so quickly that I didn't even consider the consequences. I started in June and was on the varsity golf team by the end of the summer. I hit 400–600 balls at the driving range every day and I played at least two rounds of 18 holes each day. I broke 80 sometime in September and was second seed on the team.

After golf season, I went back to my mother and said I no longer wanted the contract, the golf clubs, or the junior membership to the country club. What I really wanted was to have longer hair. She presented me with the contract that I had signed which stated that I would wear my hair the way she liked it until I graduated from high school. She was not willing to re-negotiate. That's how it was with me. When something had my attention, it had my completely undivided, all encompassing attention. Unfortunately, this meant that I sometimes missed the fine print, and had to face the consequences.

My parents took me to church regularly, almost from the moment I was born. When I was five years old, the only Christmas present I wanted was a leather cover for my Bible, and nothing else. My mother had one for her Bible and I wanted to emulate her. Fitting in and being a part of church was important to me, but I really didn't have a good understanding of the true meaning of my commitment. As a young teenager on the Outer Banks, I was a charter member of our fledgling church. I rode my bike from house to house in our neighborhood and invited families to attend church services. I was an active member of our quickly expanding youth group.

After the move to Franklin, VA, I really lost touch with God. I wasn't happy with the move and I was disillusioned with my parents' divorce. When my mother and stepfather found a church to attend, I wanted no part in it. I attended church only when forced to do so, and most of the time, that was only for special occasions. I became more focused on sports, and less on my spiritual life.

I enjoyed the attention I received and the satisfaction I got from being physically challenged. I enjoyed the competition of participating in sports, and most of all, I enjoyed the thrill of winning. All my life, I had been the biggest fish in a little pond; my boundaries were familiar and my choices were safe. That all changed when I went to college.

Chapter 2

Freedom

Radford University—Fall, 1997

I remember seeing the sign for Radford University while traveling down Interstate 81, on the day my college career would begin. I felt butterflies in my stomach as we took Exit 109, realizing that it was only a matter of hours before I would be saying goodbye to my parents for the first time.

Freedom at last, I thought. Also, *who would pack my lunches, drag me out of bed and force me to class, make me get a good night's sleep, and most importantly keep me on a straight path?*

The thought of independence was scary, but at the same time awesome.

Yes, it was time for the baby bird to leave the nest.

We drove through campus trying to locate a parking place close to my dorm building. After parking in the best location we could find, a grassy median in the middle of the road, we went to find where I could register, get my room assignment, and key. While waiting in line next to the window, I looked out at the campus. I was in a daze staring out the window watching countless other kids in the same boat as me, saying goodbye to their parents. Some kids were genuinely upset and didn't want to let their parents leave. Others were gesturing to their fathers to drag their crying mothers away so they could begin their long awaited college life. I knew how emotional my mother would get, so I wanted to get settled in as fast as possible and be done with goodbyes.

We entered my three-story brick dorm and located the room where I would be staying. I have to admit that I always visualized my college dorm room as being big and luxurious. When I walked in my initial thought was, *This is it? No way, there has to be more to it than this.*

The room I was standing in was by far smaller than any other room I had ever lived in. I then realized that I would also have to share it with a roommate. Seeing the look on my face, my mother quickly saw her final opportunity to try and keep her baby bird in the nest.

"You can always live at home and go to community college," she said.

Thinking of that alternative I quickly answered,

"No, no this will do. In fact, it's perfect!"

In that instant, that little room quickly became my new home, and after a few hours of organizing things the way my mother insisted, we said our goodbyes. My stepfather pried away my mother's arms, which were deadlocked around me, and they went on their way. I watched them through my window as they got in their car and drove away.

I then sat on my bed with my hands interlocked, my head held down, and taking long deep breaths thinking out loud to myself,

"This is it, Skinner. Are you ready for it my man?"

I realized from that point on, I would be making the majority of decisions on my own. Scary thought! In fact, looking back now, I don't feel that I was ready for this huge step. I was seventeen years young and naive to the world.

Then I began to analyze my situation from this perspective.

I'm all alone, with no parents, no adult supervision, and living on a college campus with 9,000 other kids. I felt a bit overwhelmed.

Wait a minute Skinner! I suddenly thought about the bright side. *A little over half of the students on campus are GIRLS!*

The ladies always intrigued me. I know some of you may be thinking, "What a typical guy!" Well, to be honest, I *was* typical, but you have to understand I was a seventeen-year-old man in his prime and this was an ideal situation for me. I immediately jumped up, understanding this scenario, and began jumping and dancing around the room for joy.

These will definitely be the best days of my life, I thought.

After minutes of sitting around daydreaming of fun times to come, I got myself together and decided to take a shower to freshen up before my roommate arrived. Now I must admit to you that I wasn't really looking forward to meeting my roommate for the first time. I didn't have a very good first impression of him. You see, my mom bugged me for weeks to call this guy to figure out what we needed to bring for the room. After enough nagging from Mom, I finally decided to call him and see what he was all about. I remember before dialing the phone number thinking to myself, *I hope this guy is not a complete dork! No personality, no taste in music, no interest in sports, socializing, girls…*

All these things were important to me and I hoped we would get along. I dialed the number and when he answered the phone I took a deep breath and proceeded to introduce myself.

"Hello, I am Chris Skinner, your roommate for the fall semester."

"Hey man, I am Josh," he said.

Okay, that was good. He sounded like a pretty cool guy so I began asking him what my mom had instructed me to ask.

"I need to find out what you will bring and what I need to bring for our dorm room." Now keep in mind that this was our first time in contact with each other.

Josh quickly interrupted me,

"Hey man, I've got some friends over right now and we are cooking hot dogs. Can I call you some other time?"

Surprised, I hung up the phone and thought, *Hot dogs! Are you kidding me? This guy can't even talk about school for five minutes. He has no respect.*

Because she was being a typical parent and blatantly eavesdropping, my mother heard me hang up. She walked in the room with perfect timing and asked,

"How did it go?"

"I'm not calling that guy again! I don't care what he brings." I then told my mother what happen.

I was pretty fired up at that time, but little did I know that Josh and I were alike in many ways. We both liked living life one day at a time, hanging out with friends in our comfort zones, having deep conversations, analyzing everything, and not worrying about things until we absolutely had to. I sure didn't like the kid right off the bat, but he would eventually become one of my best friends for life.

Our mothers ended up calling each other and figuring out what we needed to bring to school between them. Of course, this was exactly what both Josh and I wanted to happen in the first place.

"Parents, if they would just listen to us once in a while," Josh and I would often say. We considered ourselves masters of manipulation, and thought it was great.

When I got out of the shower I heard someone rumbling around in my room. I opened that bathroom door standing with just a towel around my waist, when I saw Josh for the first time. He didn't look anything like the mental picture I had of him. He was a slender guy standing about five foot, ten inches and weighing about one hundred and twenty pounds, at the most. His hair was black and curly, a 'fro that went every which way. He reminded me of a miniature version Kramer from the sitcom, *Seinfeld*.

This should be interesting, I thought.

After the traditional introduction and, of course, putting my clothes on, I began helping him move in, which didn't take very long. I couldn't believe what this guy had brought to school. It was close to nothing. He had his computer, TV, radio, a couple of pairs of blue jeans, and no more than ten shirts.

"This is it? This is all you brought?" I asked.

"Yup, this is all I need my man," he replied contentedly.

I noticed he was a lot like me dealing with his mom. He was hurrying her out the door to feel that first taste of freedom. Not that we don't love our mothers, because we do, unconditionally. I think Josh and I were both ready to make our own rules. Now I know why our moms cried so much.

When the coast was clear, only four words came to mind, "let the games begin." I strolled over to the stereo to turn some music on to liven things up a bit. Now keep in mind, choice of music is very important to create a bond between two guys, and I didn't have any idea what type of music Josh listened to. I took a breath and prayed that we wouldn't have a conflict of interest in music. This could put a damper on things.

"Do you mind if I put on a CD?" I asked.

"Sure, what kind of music?" he asked the million dollar question.

"What about Sublime?" I asked and then paused, awaiting the answer of the crucial question.

"Absolutely, I love Sublime," he said nodding his head. At that moment, we looked each other and smiled. We both realized that we were in for an awesome year.

After getting acquainted with our other suitemates, Anthony, Ryan, Jason, and Mike, we all decided to christen the town with our presence. It seemed like that was the plan for most freshman that first weekend. We didn't know exactly where any of the parties were, so we decided to walk around and listen for loud music. Our group met up with several other freshmen, looking for a good time. Before long, we had formed a freshman entourage, or as Josh liked to call it, a posse. Just picture this in your mind for a minute, a group of about thirty kids, all seventeen to eighteen years old, walking around knocking on doors at random and asking if they could come in and hang out. That's what we did, as ridiculous as it seems now.

In high school, we would try to find people whose parents where out of town, so we could use their house as a place to hang out and party with friends. At college, *everybody's* parents were out of town, all the time. This was the culmination of our teenage dreams, to have multiple choices and to party like rock stars with absolutely no curfew. We had arrived.

Chapter 3

First College Party

I will always remember that first party at Radford. We could hear the thumping of the music from almost a block away. You might have thought there was an earthquake by the way the ground and the house was shaking from the bass of the music.

"There it is; that's the one," I said stepping out assuming the leading position of the pack. I strolled up to the door confidently and knocked. A decent-sized guy answered the door. He had shaggy brown hair and was wearing a hat with two crossed lacrosse sticks. Underneath the sticks were the words "Radford Lacrosse."

"Five bucks to get in. Then all the punch and beer you can drink," he said, a salesman selling his product.

Wow! What a deal! We can get completely trashed for five dollars, I thought as I quickly scurried through my wallet and handed him five dollars.

As I walked into the house, I noticed the putrid smell of mold, mildew, beer and sweat. I assumed it was from so many people packed in each room like sardines dancing around, spilling beer all over each other and generating body heat from being so close together. I wondered just how many people had partied in this house over the years. You could almost picture the legacy of this house and the countless parties that had been thrown here in the past.

When I think about it now, it really doesn't make much sense. Everyone was dressed to impress, but they were dancing around on a basement floor covered with mud, stale beer, and vomit. People were slamming into each other with every move, sweating miserably, and drinking the worst, cheapest beer possible. Some people might wonder how that could possibly be considered a good time. Back then, we not only considered it a good time, we considered it paradise.

We all assembled inside and made our way to the corner where the alcohol was being served so professionally.

"Punch or beer?" asked another decent-sized guy wearing a white Lacrosse hat.

"Give me a beer," I said proudly, as if I had been going to bars for years. The next thing I knew, there was an ice-cold Milwaukee's Best in my hand, opened and ready to drink. I was impressed with the nice Lacrosse guy who took the time to open it up for me before handing it to me. I didn't know at that time, but this is a common technique used by college party hosts to conserve beer. Taking time to chat with everyone while opening their beer cans was a way of killing time, which cuts down on the number of beers served. Our posse got together against the wall and smiled at each other as we slurped down our beers. I looked around and couldn't believe how many girls were on the dance floor. It was just like a scene out of the movie *Animal House*.

After a few beers were in my system, I suddenly felt the confidence, a.k.a. alcohol, running through my veins and was sucked out onto the dance floor. Before I knew it, I was dancing all around. I felt two hands wrap around me from behind and someone began dancing with me in perfect tempo. I turned around and it didn't take me more than a second to accept the invitation to dance with this cute, young college girl. Without a word said, we were hip-to-hip, super-glued together and moving in ways I can't even begin to describe. It was crowded, so it was hard to keep our rhythm, but we somehow managed.

Looking over the girl's shoulder, I saw my friends' heads shaking with approval and giving me the thumbs up. The girl's hot sweaty cheek rubbed against mine, and we began to kiss. I couldn't believe it! My first party at college, my first dance with a college girl, and I was making out right in the middle of everyone. It was really happening. I didn't get the girl's name when the song ended. I tried to start a conversation with her, but she just turned around and walked away. I was shocked. We had just made out in front of everyone, and she was walking away, no strings attached.

Wow, college is UNBELIEVABLE! I thought to myself.

I walked back over to my friends with a cocky smile, and a pimp lean in my walk, thinking I can definitely get used to this college atmosphere. Walking up, they all gave me high fives saying things like, "You're the man, Skinner!"

Everything was going great, the music was pumping, the party was slamming, and I had already met a girl who just couldn't resist me. Or so I thought in my innocence. I never considered the possibility that the girl was trying to make a certain friend of hers jealous. Yep, you guessed it. Apparently, the girl was trying to make a certain guy friend of hers angry.

He was not only just *some guy*; he was a pretty decent-sized guy in a white Lacrosse hat. Are you catching on to what is happening here? In a matter of seconds, my perspective about the slamming party, the girl who couldn't resist me, and the nice guys in the white hats was dramatically reversed.

Suddenly, I was pinned against the wall and surrounded by at least ten nice guys wearing white Lacrosse hats. Except now they didn't seem so nice. One of the guys was screaming in my face and poking my chest with his index finger. The rest of them stood in a semi-circle around me with their teeth clenched tightly, arms crossed, and not saying a word.

"What's going on man?" I asked. I began to fear for my safety.

"You stole my teammates sunglasses," the guy yelled.

"No, man, it wasn't me. I don't know what you're talking about," I said. I had figured out what was going on. You see, one of the Lacrosse guys apparently liked the girl that I had danced with and kissed. When he saw that one of his teammates was flipping out about someone stealing his sunglasses, he saw the perfect opportunity to take his anger out on me. Lucky me. My first party, the first girl I meet, and here I was about to get my teeth kicked in by an entire Lacrosse team because of a jealous, psychopathic boyfriend!

I still don't know how I survived that night. Somehow, I managed to sneak out the door untouched and unharmed. I don't think I have ever run so fast in my life as I did that night, back to my dorm room. I still wonder today if that girl ever knew exactly what she put me through.

After talking things over with my suitemates all day Sunday, we came up with the conclusion that the school was big enough that I wouldn't have to worry about running into any of those guys again. And even if I did, they wouldn't remember who I was, since everyone was so drunk and it was so dark. I was in for a rude awakening.

Chapter 4

Protection Is The Plan

After my first day of class, my suitemates and I met in the cafeteria for lunch. We laughed and joked around about the weekend, finished our lunch, and started to make our way out of the cafeteria. As I turned the corner, I stood face-to-face with the same Lacrosse guys from the weekend. They were coming in to eat just as we were leaving. My heart started beating really fast as I put my head down and tried to sneak out without being recognized. I kept telling myself they would never remember me. Then I realized that I was sadly mistaken when a couple of guys walked by me bumping their shoulders into mine and mumbling some words that I would rather not repeat. To put it in a PG rated way, they were saying, "watch your back."

At this point I knew something had to be done if I didn't want to be tormented for the remainder of my first semester. I couldn't put my finger on what it was. I had heard about fraternities in high school, and have seen movies about them, but I really had no clue of what they were all about. It seems almost uncanny to me the way things worked out from this point on.

A couple of days later, while I was walking around campus hoping I wouldn't run into the Lacrosse team, I saw a group of guys sitting in the middle of the campus where the fraternities and sororities hung out during the day. These guys stood out to me because they were being loud and obnoxious, teasing people who walked by. It seemed like they controlled the area just by their presence. I noticed people actually walking the long way around campus so they didn't have to walk by them and risk being called out or put in the spotlight.

My initial thought was that these guys were jerks and very intimidating. After a closer look, I noticed that there were all sorts of girls sitting around with them, laughing and flirting.

Hmm, they must be doing something right to have all those girls hanging around, I thought.

Like I told you, girls always intrigued me, and that interest always seemed to get me into trouble. The guys seemed like the center of attention and I have to admit, I kind of envied that. One of the guys noticed that I was checking them out and he stood up, staring directly at me, and walked toward me.

Oh great Skinner, just what you need, another group of guys wanting to kick your teeth in, I thought as he came closer and closer with this serious look on his face. I mean these guys weren't just decent-sized fellows like the Lacrosse boys. They were downright huge. The guy approaching, in particular, looked sort of like the Incredible Hulk. Luckily, I just happened to be walking with two nice looking girls from my high school, and some other girls we had met earlier that day.

He walked right up to me not cracking a smile and said, "Hey man, how's it going? My name is Little."

I had no idea how his name could be Little. The man's biceps were bursting out of his shirt.

"We are having a party tonight. You should come," he said as he reached his hand out toward me and handed me a business card.

"And Uh, don't forget to bring all your lovely lady friends," he added charmingly.

And that was it. That's all he said. He turned around and walked back assuming position with his guys. I looked down at the card he had given me and it had some funny looking Greek letters on it. Also, just underneath the letters, it had a giant Bulldog crossing WWF-worthy arms and a phrase that read, "RUSH, but only if you're strong to belong." On the back of the card was an address of the fraternity house where the party was being held.

I almost threw the card away, when suddenly a light bulb switched on in my brain.

Protection! I thought to myself as I pictured the Lacrosse team beating my brains in with their sticks for the rest of the semester. If I could get in with these frat guys, I would be set for the rest of my college career. I thought even the Lacrosse guys wouldn't mess with this group of monsters. I knew being the arrogant, scrawny, loud mouth kid that I was in those days made it very probable I would need some protection at some point in time. Especially since after just one weekend in Radford and my first party, I already had a whole team of guys wanting to beat me up. I figured this might be a perfect opportunity to meet some new friends, and not just ordinary friends, either. Big intimidating friends that would be absolutely perfect for getting my back in sticky situations.

With my brilliant plan developing, I looked over at the girls with my perfected puppy dog face and pleaded.

"Come on girls, don't you want to go to the party with me?"

They weren't too sure at first, but after I explained my situation and added a little bit of the Skinner charm, they agreed to join me.

Thank the Lord for girls, I thought, grinning. Things were falling into place perfectly.

Chapter 5

Frat Party

When we arrived at the party that night, it was slamming. We had no problems finding the place because of the mobs of people milling around the house. By the time we made it to the door, there were a couple of huge guys standing there telling people that the party was cut off. They weren't letting any more people in. I couldn't believe that the house was already maxed out.

The girls, my roommate Josh, and I paused for a second to think of an alternative. They were ready to turn around and head back, especially Josh. It had taken forever to convince him to come along. He was always content with just hanging out in the room drinking, listening to music, and playing video games. I hated the fact that I had dragged all of these people out with me and now we couldn't even get in. Acting like I had some sort of connections, I tried to calm the crew down

"Hang on a second. Let me see what I can do," I said, thinking I could charm my way in as usual.

I started walking over to the guys with the Rush card that the guy called Little had given me in my back pocket. One of the guys at the door said,

"Hey man, I already told you we are cut off."

I had a brief feeling of failure as I glanced over at my friends and saw the look of disappointment and discomfort on their faces when they overheard his words. I knew I had to do something fast, because I saw my friends losing faith in me.

At that point, my manipulation skills kicked in, and I literally played the only card I had. I quickly took it out of my pocket and stared at it, hoping it would help us get into the party. I thought about how many of these cards they could have possibly passed out.

It couldn't have been that many, or at least not as many as people in the house, I thought.

I handed the card to the monstrous guys and said with confidence,

"Hey fellows, a guy named Little gave me this card. He asked me to show up and bring these ladies with me."

Not saying a word to me, the guys began yelling in the house to get Little. My guess was that they wanted to see if my story checked out. Even though I was a little nervous and didn't even know if this guy would remember who I was, I still managed to look over to my friends give them a wink and a thumbs up. I bet they were thinking, "yeah right, is this guy for real? We are never getting in that house." I knew that if this fell through on me, I would never hear the end of it, but I was a trooper and stood my ground.

When Little came to the door, I smiled and said, "What's up man," extending my hand as if we knew each other. I was stalling a little to allow his mind to process and remember me.

For a second, I thought I was toast judging by the look on his face, when suddenly he said, "Oh yeah, the kid with all the girls."

Relieved, I let out a sigh and said, "Yup that's me."

"Well, did you bring them with you?" he followed up.

"Of course man, they are right over there," I said pointing toward them. Oh yeah, this was going to work.

"What is your name?" he asked.

"Chris Skinner," I told him.

He turned towards the other guys and said,

"Hey fellows, this is Skinner. He is thinking about rushing this semester."

Then he looked back at me along with all the other guys, waiting for my positive response.

I thought to myself, I *don't ever remember saying I was going to rush, but whatever. It seems to be working so I'll go along with it.*

"Well, Ye…Yeah. I am, " I said, just to go with the flow.

After that it was all good. The guys suddenly turned and came towards me saying,

"Well why didn't you say so? Come on in and have a good time."

With victory written all over my face, I turned to my friends and waived for them to come in.

"Right this way, ladies. Enjoy yourself and let us know if there's anything you need," one of the guys said as my friends walked through the door.

I just smiled as they walked by, one by one, each with a look of disbelief on their face. My friends started working their way around the party, as I stood talking with the big fraternity brothers for a while.

Little put his arm around me and took me to a separate room that he said was called "The brother room." He explained how this was a privilege because only brothers of the fraternity and selected guests were allowed in. It finally hit me that this was one of those fraternities like you see on TV and in movies. That explained what those funny looking letters on the card were. They really *were* Greek letters.

My curiosity level increased, and I began asking questions. Anyone who knows me can tell you I always ask tons of questions. In fact, my friend Robin says that I ask more questions then Alex Trebek from the show *Jeopardy*. I get it from my mom. She always told me that no question is a dumb question and if you don't know something, it's much better to ask. So I started firing away asking this guy Little all kinds of questions. What do the letters stand for? What are their colors? How many brothers are there? How long is the pledge period? I asked all kinds of basic questions about the organization.

I noticed that he was very proud of the fraternity, as well as their motto that was plastered all over their posters, "strong to belong." I really liked the sound of the motto. I always considered myself a strong person and I usually fit in where ever I am. I began wondering if I had what it took, if I was strong to belong. I was sucked right in to this macho way of thinking. I'm telling you, it really wasn't hard to do in the midst of all that excitement, the partying, the challenge, and the peer pressure. The most important issue to me at the time, besides the back up from monsters, were the girls. Girls really seemed to like all the guys with the letters on their chest. These were the wrong things for me to focus on, I realize, but they were just too appealing for a seventeen year old man to turn down.

The brothers handed me a notebook with a list of several names and numbers. They asked me to sign my name on the page, and to include some information about me such as my year in school, telephone number, age, and so forth. It was general information so the brothers could find out a little bit about us, and to keep track of our contact information in case they wanted us to rush. The whole process was kind of funny. At this point, I still wasn't *really* considering pledging. I was just going along with all the excitement, and enjoying the perks that the fraternity gave to potential pledges.

The night went on and we had a blast. My posse was treated as if we were already part of the family. After saying goodbye to at least twenty brothers that I had met, my friends and I called it quits and headed home.

Walking home that night, we laughed about how we got into the party, and how we were treated like royalty all night. I was on cloud nine. One of my friends asked,

"Hey Skinner, are you seriously thinking about pledging that fraternity?"

"I don't think so. I mean it looks fun and I kind of want to, but I know my mom would never go for it."

You see, my older brother had joined a fraternity at UNCW a couple of years before, so my mom knew what fraternities were all about. My brother always seemed to have a way of ruining things that I might want to do before I ever got a chance to do them. He would experience them first, test the waters, screw up somehow, and make my mother alert to these situations. This made it very hard for me to persuade her to see anything from my point of view. We couldn't agree on certain things, because she knew what could, and most likely would, happen if I followed in my brother's footsteps. She knew our personalities too well, and she knew just how similar our thought processes could be. She understood how we made the majority of our decisions. I think I can speak for my brother when I say that we have both made some really dumb decisions. Poor Mom.

When I spoke to my mother on Sunday, I didn't even mention my interest in a fraternity. I was not in the mood for a long lecture on being responsible and making good decisions.

Chapter 6

To Pledge Or Not To Pledge

The next couple of weeks passed and I became increasingly comfortable with my new college life and routine. One afternoon Josh and I were sitting around playing video games, our competitive ritual, when the phone rang. Josh usually answered the phone and screened phone calls for me.

Sometimes I would meet girls at parties, and I would give them my number while intoxicated. Then, when they called, I didn't want to talk to them. I know this sounds terrible. Josh would tell the girls that I wasn't in, and then get mad at me for asking him to do that. He called me a dirtball.

Dirtball was an understatement. I listened closely to Josh as he answered the phone trying to figure out who was calling, so I could give the nod. I heard Josh say,

"Hello…Oh hey, how's it going man?"

Once I knew that it was a guy, I felt relieved and gave Josh a nod indicating I was available if the call was for me.

"No…No. This is Josh, Skinner's roommate. Hold on a sec, he's right here."

He handed me the phone, gesturing that he had no clue who the caller was.

"Hello," I said confidently.

"Skinner, hey man, this is Bailey calling from the fraternity house." At first I was a little confused, but then it came to me. I remembered signing the rush sheet at their party.

"Oh hey, how's it going?" I asked, starting to panic. I knew he was calling about pledging and I still had no clue what I was going to do.

"Well, we noticed you missed the first two rushes so I was calling to inform you that tonight is our final, closed rush," he said. There was a slight pause as he waited for feedback.

"Aww man, thanks for calling. I didn't know where they were being held, or who to get in touch with," I blatantly lied. I felt the peer pressure increase.

"Well, look man, no worries. I'll come by your room and pick you up in about an hour. That way you won't have to find the house. Is that cool?" He knew I would be there for sure, this time. It was a clever move on his part.

"Sure. Sounds good. See you then." I said. I didn't really want to go with him, but I kept envisioning Lacrosse sticks slamming across my face.

I guess the expression on my face said it all after I hung the phone up. Josh was concerned.

"What is the matter? Was that the fraternity guys? Are you going to pledge?"

He bombarded me with questions while I silently walked to my closet in a daze. I selected something that I thought would be appropriate to wear.

"I am going to the final rush, but I'm still not sure if I'll pledge," I answered honestly. It was the truth. I still wasn't planning on pledging. I was going with the flow like I always did, without considering the consequences.

One hour later, there was a knock on the door. I yelled, "Come in" and the door slowly opened. There stood an average sized guy. Not as intimidating as the other brothers I had met, but good-looking and very athletic. This set me at ease; I wasn't huge either, but I considered myself good-looking and athletic.

"Chris Skinner," he said, looking in my direction.

"That would be me," I said as I rose to shake his hand.

"Bailey here. Nice to meet you," he said, shaking my hand with a firm grip.

Huh, maybe I could do this fraternity thing, I thought as I followed Bailey down the stairs out the door and into his car.

We didn't say much at all during the car ride, just a typical small talk conversation—Where are you from? Any brothers and sisters? Hobbies? And so on. Before I knew it, we pulled into the driveway of the fraternity house and were on the way in.

I noticed the yard as we walked toward the door. It was completely trashed with smashed beer cans, empty plastic cups, cigarette butts, and dirty clothes. Leftovers from a previous party. I'm not someone who normally cares about clutter, but this was too much even for me.

The door of the house was wide open, as if the house dared someone to enter unbidden. The outside of the house basically looked like a dump, and it didn't get much better when I walked through the door. I noticed holes in the walls that I assumed people had punched during fights. There were numerous, elaborately decorated paddles hanging on the wall with names listed on each of them. A giant purple and black flag hung on another wall, proudly displaying the fraternity's Greek letters. This banner seemed to be a strategic attempt to make the place look somewhat decent.

There were a couple of sofas in the living room with chunks missing from the cushions. A massive, ferocious pit bull was sitting on one of them. His mouth was full of razor sharp fangs. I quickly surmised how the holes were made. The floors were tile, covered in mud, beer, spit and vomit. To top it off, there was a tapped keg in the corner of the kitchen. It was surrounded by about forty oversized fraternity brothers who all looked like they ate small children for lunch. It is safe to say that at this point, I was just a bit overwhelmed. I was not feeling any good vibes.

I continued to feel overwhelmed until I was introduced to the president of the fraternity, Clegg. He was another decent-sized guy who stood about six foot, three inches and weighed about one hundred ninety pounds. Now this guy had a way with words. I think Clegg could've talked a Catholic schoolgirl into pledging that fraternity. He carried himself in a very smooth, professional, confident, and downright arrogant way. I admit it; I really liked the guy, and the way he operated, from the beginning. I mean, he fired me up and eventually talked me into pledging that night. He conned a conman, and he reminded me a lot of myself.

For the next half hour, Clegg took me through the entire fraternity's history, at the same time showing me around the house and introducing me to different brothers. I could tell that he had a real passion and was very proud of this organization. I am always impressed with people who are truly passionate about something.

After the guided tour, he took me to a room and explained to me that they had already interviewed the other potential pledges. Since I had missed the first two rushes, I would have to give a live interview that night, standing in front of the entire fraternity.

He asked me to wait in a specific room while he gathered all of the boys together. I know I've said that I love being the center of attention, but I suddenly began to feel very nervous and intimidated. The brothers began to file into the room one-by-one, all wearing a solemn expression void of any emotion. They seemed very serious about their selection process. I felt like I was trying out for the varsity basketball team all over again, and it was time to hear if I made the cut. As the last brothers came trickling through the door, my confident Chris Skinner mode kicked in, and I began psyching myself up mentally.

You're the man. Come on Skinner, just be yourself.

After all the guys were assembled in the room, they placed a video camera directly in front of me. The room quieted. Clegg pulled up a chair in front of me, and began asking questions. It was a little nerve-wracking at first. I had no idea what kind of questions they planned to ask. Right off the bat, Clegg threw me a funny, off-the-wall question that caught me completely off guard. I tried to answer as seriously as possible, but it was no use. The whole room burst into laughter, including me. After the laughter, my pre-game jitters were pretty much gone. I fired away, answering each question with confidence and a little humor, just like I was talking to a bunch of friends. When the interview was completed, Clegg asked me to go downstairs and wait with the rest of the potential pledges while the brothers went through their selection process.

When I went downstairs I noticed the smell again. The pungent combination of sweat, beer, vomit, mold and mildew is certainly distinctive. I never could get used to that smell. The stinky old basement was filled with guys standing around, nervously waiting to see if they got a bid into the fraternity. I remember one guy came up to me and asked if I was a brother. I answered no, and explained that I was unable to make the first two rushes and I had just finished my interview upstairs. I started conversations with some guys, who told me how nervous they were and how much they wanted a bid. I was pretty much in a daze, myself. I didn't know why I was there, and I didn't know what to think. I was just going with the flow as usual.

The brothers came downstairs and took one potential pledge at a time upstairs to let them know if they had made the cut. There were fewer and fewer guys around me by the minute. I thought that maybe they saved all the guys who wouldn't get a bid for last, so they could come down and tell all of us at once. The idea offended me, because I was very competitive (and arrogant if you haven't already noticed) and felt like I was much cooler than most of the candidates who had gone upstairs. Before I knew it, I was all fired up and sweating the decision just like all the other guys. I got sucked right in. There were only three guys left when Clegg came downstairs with a very solemn, straightforward face. He stood there for a second, then looked at me.

"Skinner, come on up man."

For a second I thought, *Well maybe they aren't going to dump me.*

I have been known to over-analyze situations. Throughout my life, this tendency has caused me more than a few problems. I thought about Clegg's serious expression.

I know that look, I repeated to myself over and over.

It was the look that people have when they need to tell you some bad news, but don't really want to.

They are going to cut me, I thought, getting mad. I followed Clegg up the stairs.

I was all worked up by the time I reached the top stair. I remember glancing around the corner and seeing the entire fraternity circled around the edge of a room. They were completely silent with their mouths closed, their teeth clenched, and their eyes focused directly at me. I put my head down and avoided direct eye contact with everyone, as if I were in court being convicted of a murder.

This definitely cannot be good, I thought. *This is why I didn't want to come here in the first place!* My inner voice began to whine like a baby.

Clegg led me to the center of the room. He stood directly in front of me with a notebook in his hand, looked me in the eyes, and spoke.

"As you know, we, the brothers take great pride in making our selection in pledges and potential brothers." His tone was sincere.

Oh great, I thought, *he's going to try to make it seem as if it was very difficult to choose between us and then let me down easy.*

"We had an outrageous amount of potential pledges come out this semester, which of course made the selection process even more difficult," he continued.

Blah, blah, blah. I said to myself, *Why don't you just spare me the time and give me the news? We are sorry we can't take you this semester, but feel free to come out again next time.* This noisy internal rant almost made me miss Clegg's punch line.

"After talking over your interview, we would like to offer you a bid into our fraternity," he finished with a smile.

I guess the look on my face showed how surprised I was. He repeated himself.

"Skinner do you accept the bid?"

Relieved, I regained my composure.

"Yeah, sure why not?"

I was trying to play it smooth, as if I wasn't sweating the decision. As soon as the words came out of my mouth, all the guys tackled me at once. We fell onto the floor screaming and yelling with excitement. It felt like we had just won game seven of the World Series. Clegg handed me a black shirt with little purple and gray letters on the left side.

They were all screaming, "Put it on." Their enthusiasm made it difficult for me to follow their demand. It was almost impossible to put on the shirt because they kept pushing me around.

And that's exactly how it happened. One moment I was sitting in my dorm playing video games with total freedom and plenty of time, and a couple of hours later, I was a full-fledged pledge to a fraternity with no idea what was in store. It was nice to know that the fraternity wanted to give me the chance to join them. I was excited about this, and relieved. My worries about the whole Lacrosse team situation were gone. All I had to do now was make it through the semester as a pledge and become a brother. After that, I would be untouchable. How hard could it be?

How hard? Now there's a trick question. The real question to ask is, "how naive can a seventeen-year-old be?"

The brothers put the pledges together in one room, introduced us briefly, and then began explaining the rules and regulations of pledging. I was actually very impressed. The rules, surprisingly, seemed very structured and well thought out.

The founders of the fraternity must have put a lot time and effort into putting this organization together, I thought.

You see, their rules sounded legitimate, and even sensible. For example, there would be absolutely no drinking from Sunday through Thursday. On these nights, we had to attend two hours of mandatory study hall, with no exceptions. We had mandatory work out hours throughout the week, and were expected to try and be as healthy as possible. We were to avoid fast food, soda, and tobacco products. We were to wear a shirt and tie to class every Monday, and our pledge shirts on Wednesdays. It didn't sound like such a bad idea after all. To tell the truth, there was no way I would study two hours a night, or work out in a gym five days a week, without being forced to do so. And eating right and wearing a shirt and tie to class? No way. It just wasn't in me.

After listening to the rules, I thought to myself,

I don't understand why my mother is so against this, when it seems like it will help me more than anything. It just doesn't make sense.

There are two phrases that come to mind when I think back to my pledging experience. You may have them heard once or twice in your life—"Don't judge a book by its cover," and "What you see isn't always what you get." Pledging seemed like a great idea for many reasons, but it turns out that Mom was right about fraternities, after all.

Now before I go any further, I want to make it clear that I mean no disrespect towards the fraternity. There were a lot of good guys in the organization who cared about the rules and regulations, and acted accordingly. I still respect those men to this day. Unfortunately, there were plenty of "bad apples," who spoiled things for everyone. You know what I'm talking about. It happens in any large group you put together. There is always someone disagreeing, complaining, breaking the rules, and making things difficult for everyone else.

For the next twelve weeks, I did nothing but eat, breathe, and sleep fraternity. I felt like I was in basic training for the Army, except I had forty-three drill sergeants. Pledges were treated like little gophers, constantly running errands for people, cleaning houses, washing dishes, washing cars, mopping floors, bringing food, giving rides, walking dogs, and performing any and all tasks that the brothers told us to do. I learned that this was one of the perks of making it through pledging and becoming a brother. Once you became a brother, you had little slaves to do the dirty work for you. That was what I focused on, as a reward to keep myself going, but I promised myself I would not get carried away with the power like some of the guys did.

I focused my undivided attention on the tasks of pledging. After completing my twelve weeks of slavery, pledging was over and I became a brother. I remember waking up the morning after I became a brother and not knowing what to do with myself. While I was pledging, I never had enough time to do anything. Now, as a brother, I had too much time to do everything. That was when the problems began.

Chapter 7

A Time For Consequences

You may have noticed that I didn't mention school while describing my twelve weeks as a pledge. When I woke up to reality, I realized I had only two weeks of the semester left and I had no idea what type of grades I was getting that semester. On top of that, I never told my mother that I was pledging. When she asked about my classes, I always answered, "I'm doing good Mom, don't worry about it. Trust me." This sort of talk would become less and less effective, not to mention less and less truthful, as my college career unfolded. The long-term consequences of deceiving my mom were much less important to me than the immediate consequences I could expect if I failed my classes because I joined a fraternity.

I buckled down, which in this case meant that I opened my books for the first time, and I began studying for final exams. I studied all day and night for two weeks, trying to learn everything I missed. I felt like I did a pretty decent job, considering it was my first time studying for the entire semester. However, I didn't expect my grades to be so hot.

Throughout Christmas break, I stayed as optimistic as I could, for as long as I could, about my grades. My family eagerly awaited the arrival of my grades. The day they came in the mail was the day that I had been dreading. The mailman knocked on the door and handed my mother a stack of mail. I remember clenching my teeth, taking deep breaths, and praying for one more day of reprieve from reality.

My mother sorted through the mail, looking each letter

over carefully. She pulled a letter from the stack and looked up at me.

"Chris, I think your grades are here."

Her voice sounded like the principal on *Charlie Brown*, "Wha, wha wha wha WHA!"

She opened the letter, anxious to see what her money had paid for that semester. I was not as eager. When I saw her smile slowly drop to a frown, and her skin turn bright red, like it always did when I had done something really wrong, I began preparing myself. It would be an all out battle. Head to head. Mother against son. We were milliseconds from the first skirmish.

I was lucky; I had used the time before the grades arrived to work on explanations and several different plans of attack. One point for my side. On the other hand, I still had no idea what my grades were. I didn't know exactly how deep of a hole I had to get myself out of. I knew it was pretty deep when my mother walked past me, handed me my grades, and said, "in the kitchen. Now."

I unfolded the piece of paper and looked down at my grades. My eyes were drawn to the cumulative grade point average (GPA). I was honestly relieved to discover that I had earned a 2.1 GPA. It meant that I had passed for the semester, but just barely. At Radford you must keep a 2.0 GPA or you get placed on academic probation.

Okay, I can work with this. I felt relieved, but remembered to hold my head down and look upset as I walked into the kitchen. I was going to attempt a peace treaty. I can't remember exactly what was said at that table. All I remember was the tone of my mom's voice, and the physical expressions of disappointment on her face. Both were evidence of her disappointment. It definitely was not a good scenario. I sat there with my head down, taking every blow like a man, until she finished venting.

When it was my turn to explain, I started by telling her the truth about pledging the fraternity. At the same time, I was trying to locate the nearest fire extinguisher; flames were going to come out of my mother's ears at any moment. Before letting her start the barrage of *'I told you so's,* I quickly admitted it was unacceptable and stupid, and it wouldn't happen again. I assured her I would focus on my schoolwork and do better next time. After two or three hours of talking and working things out, my mother agreed to allow me to return to school for another semester. I figured it wouldn't be too hard to concentrate on school now that pledging was over. I was wrong.

Chapter 8

Try Again—Second Semester

When we returned to school, Josh and I found we were in similar situations. Our GPAs were similar, and so were our mothers' responses and expectations. We decided that together we would try harder and make better grades for that semester. Unfortunately, I found out that it was even harder to concentrate on school as a brother than when I was pledging. When I pledged, I had mandatory study hall hours. Now I had to make time on my own to study, which I found nearly impossible to do with my phone ringing off the hook. It seemed like there was a party or some extravagant event going on every night that I just couldn't miss. I was a social butterfly, as you have learned, and loved being the center of attention. I felt obligated to make an appearance at every social gathering. As you can imagine, this made it hard on Josh to concentrate on school. I was always nagging him to come along with me. I admit that he was much stronger than I was. He would turn me down and stay in more than half of the time.

The more I went out, the more I became addicted to the social life. The more I became addicted to the social life, the more I enjoyed getting intoxicated. There was a stretch of time in that second semester when I went out every night for a month straight and got completely trashed. When I look back at pictures taken during that semester, I wish I could reach through the photo and grab my younger self by the neck. I wish I could tell my younger self, "Get yourself straight. That is not who you are!"

Pretty soon, getting drunk every night started to bore me. It just wasn't enough to satisfy my craving for partying. I needed more. I couldn't tell you what I needed "more" of, because I didn't know myself. I was so caught up in wanting to fit in, and being the center of attention. I wanted to be the most popular freshman on campus, the guy that everyone knew—the cool guy.

What is cool, really? That is a good question; it took me years of mistakes to figure out the answer. Cool is not trying to fit in, doing things just to impress others, or trying to be somebody that you aren't. Cool is being content with who you are as a person. It is making your own decisions in any situation, at any given moment, in accordance with who you are. It's being strong enough to do what you know is right, even if it means sacrificing the way your peers feel about you. *That* is cool. And it is the exact opposite of who I was during this particular time of my life. I was acting as a follower, instead of a leader. I cared more about how I wanted to be seen than about staying true to myself and my understanding of right and wrong.

I'll give you an example of what I'm talking about. I was at a party that was really jamming off the hook. The house was packed with people sweating, drinking, dancing, and listening to loud thumping music. You get the picture—the typical fraternity party. Another fraternity hosted the party; we attended simply because we were friends with this other frat house. It's pretty stupid, but when you join a fraternity you are basically brainwashed into liking or disliking other organizations based solely on how the older brothers felt about them.

Somehow I found myself in a little room upstairs, separate from the rest of the party, with a couple of older guys. I looked up to them. I thought they were cool, and wanted to fit in and be cool, too. They were all hunched over this one guy, watching him like a pack of wolves about to feed on an injured lamb. He pulled a little plastic baggy out of his pocket and tossed it on the table. The baggy had what looked like a few tablespoons of sugar in it.

I am going to be honest with you. When I was in high school, I used a few illegal substances. I drank a little alcohol, even though I was underage, and I even tried smoking marijuana. But I had never seen cocaine until that night. As the guy spread the white powder across the table and started cutting out lines with a razor blade, I felt my stomach churning and my conscience haunting me with guilt. I started thinking back to second grade when I had the *D.A.R.E.* class that informed us about what drugs would do to your body. Despite all the guilt I was feeling in my stomach, and my uneasy conscience, when my turn came in the rotation I was unable to do the *really* cool thing.

All eyes were on me. One of the guys said, "Come on Skinner, you're up."

I must have had the word **scared** written in giant bold letters across my forehead because another guy asked bluntly, "you have done this before, haven't you?"

Making the worst possible decision, I assumed my position at the table and said with a forced smile, "Of course I've done it before. Get out of my way." I leaned over the table and imitated what the other guys had done. I jumped up in pain, holding my nose because of the intense burning of the drug.

The guys laughed, and patted me on the back with approval saying, "good stuff, huh, Skinner?"

With watering eyes and a stinging nose, I grinned and managed to say, "Yeah man, good stuff."

This was the beginning of the lowest point of my life. After that night, things quickly went downhill, like a landslide. I began to lose more and more focus in my life. I gave less and less concentration to schoolwork, God, sports, and everything positive and productive. My undivided attention, regrettably, was concentrated on socializing, partying, alcohol, and drugs. I was completely hopeless, for the first time in my life. Things were slipping away from me, and I had absolutely no control over them.

When my mother called, she would stay on the phone longer than usual. She told me that something was different about me, and she thought I needed help.

"I'm fine. I'm just a college student," I would plead with her, implying that all college students were going through and doing the same thing I was.

Maybe I began to believe it myself. It is plain and simple to me now that I was *not* just like every other college student, but I really had myself convinced. I just wouldn't admit to myself, or anyone else, that I had a problem. I was so caught up in my lifestyle, and so wrapped in my protective lies, that I actually believed that I was fine and had everything under control. Guess what? I was wrong! People try to place blame as far from them as they can, so they will never have to accept responsibility for their own actions. I always pointed the finger elsewhere when I was in trouble.

Chapter 9

A Deeper Hole

Outer Banks, NC—Summer, 1998

It became obvious that I didn't have everything under control when I received a whopping 1.6 GPA at the end of my second semester of college. I was placed on academic probation for one semester.

Fortunately, I was living and working in Nags Head, North Carolina for the summer at the time my mom received the grades. Instead of getting her death look, I received hours of loud, angry scolding over the phone. I developed a nasty migraine from that conversation. I still feel lucky that I wasn't around the house on the day she got the grades in the mail. Let's just say she was a little fired up—with complete justification.

During the first conversation on the phone my mother screamed, "you will never go back to that school again!" At the time, I didn't think it would be a good idea to argue, so I went along with all that she said to save myself from even more lecturing. I figured I would let things cool down for a while and then I would make my move.

After a couple of weeks, I polished up my persuasion tactics and started talking with my mom about school and my plans to return. I vowed to do better and promised once again to succeed if given another chance. I explained to her how the summer was helping me grow up, since I was working and paying my own bills. She asked me about alcohol and drugs. I admitted that I tried a few things, but I once again explained how I was just a normal college student and was doing what any other kid my age was doing. She didn't buy it, pleading with me to come home and seek help.

Meanwhile, I fell deeper and deeper into partying and drugs. I can assure you that it was not the type of partying and drugs that average college students were doing. It is unbelievable that I thought my behavior was normal! I still honestly felt like I had my life under control. I was wrong again, and it kept getting worse.

My mother, for the first time, stood her ground. She said no to the whole idea of returning to Radford and taking classes at New River Community College. She told me if I wanted to return to Radford University, I would have to come home for a semester and attend community college in Franklin, to prove to her I was able to make the grades.

Refusing to agree with those terms, I rebelled. I tried to figure how I could get enough money to return to Radford on my own. I was convinced that I didn't need her help to succeed. I just want to say for the record that this was the stupidest thing I've ever thought in my life. Without my mother, I am like a gun without ammo—useless.

I lost even more of my marbles when I met a girl down at the beach. Without a second thought, I packed up all my stuff and moved to Buena Vista, VA with her. I just up and left one day without telling anyone. My friends, my boss, and my family had no warning, and no idea where I was. I worked as a lifeguard at a local pool in Buena Vista, and I wasn't earning enough money to save for college tuition, books, or rent. I could barely afford to eat and put gas in my car. I was running out of time and had to figure something out quick.

Towards the end of the summer, I took a trip to Knoxville, TN to visit my grandparents and my uncle. I explained to them my situation and mentioned how eager I was to return to school and succeed. After talking things over with me, they decided to help. They were going to give me some financial support, but only enough to get my feet back on the ground. I would have enough money to pay rent and also to sign up for some community college classes. Before I left that weekend, I promised to do well in school and to repay them the money as soon as possible. Of course, they didn't want me to repay them. They loved me and wanted me to succeed. I feel pain in my heart to this day for accepting their money, even though I have long since repaid my debt. If I had been a man of my word and held up my end of the deal, things might be different.

Chapter 10

Opportunities Lost—And So Was I

Radford, VA—Fall, 1998

I returned to Radford and used the money entrusted to me to pay my bills. I never signed up for classes as I had promised. Instead I worked part-time at a deli and became a full-time partier.

The next four months of my life were a total blur. I worked three to four days a week as a delivery boy for about six hours a day, making just enough money for basic necessities. I recall rushing home after work, taking a shower, and heading straight out to a party where I would drink myself into a drunken stupor, or something worse. Drugs were always available to anyone who wanted to intensify their already altered state of consciousness.

It was an unhealthy life. The day after a party, I would sleep off the effects of the toxins. When I woke up, I would repeat the cycle. I lost weight and felt my mind and body slipping away from me, but I didn't have the sense to care. I'm very fortunate to have survived that semester of recklessness and poor decision-making.

When my probation semester was almost over, I filed an appeal in hopes of being re-admitted into Radford University. I had to fill out another admissions application, write several essays about why I should be allowed a second chance, and meet with my adviser. After dealing with all of this red tape, I was granted yet another chance to succeed.

Radford, VA—Spring, 1999

I returned to school for the spring semester psyched up, once again promising myself and everyone else that I would stay focused and succeed. You must be thinking, "for the love of Pete! I hope this guy finally gets it together."

Everything started off on the right track with my first week back. I made it to every class without much distraction. I was taking a full load of courses, which meant twelve total credit hours. However, after the first week, my focus completely vanished. I began putting things off, skipping my classes, and making up all kinds of excuses for myself. I missed two American Literature pop quizzes the second week. Giving up, I withdrew from the class. Now I was only carrying nine credit hours. As the semester crept by, I continued procrastinating, promising myself that I would buckle down towards the end of the semester.

Unfortunately, with one week left in the semester, and final exams on the way, I suddenly woke from my haze and began to panic. I knew that if my GPA was below a 2.0 at the end of this semester, I would be suspended for a full year, with a good chance of never being allowed back into Radford University.

When I realized this, I ran to my professors' offices to ask about my grades. Because I had skipped class so much, I don't think my teachers knew who I was. It was pathetic and embarrassing to say the least. I needed to get at least three Cs. I found out that I had two Fs and a C. I asked for extra credit and they pulled out the course outlines, the ones that I never bothered to read, which stated in bold letters, "absolutely no extra credit allowed."

I pleaded my case with all sorts of excuses. In the end, I would have to score an A on both my final exams just to get

Cs for the semester. I was overwhelmed considering that the final exams were cumulative, meaning they would cover all the information from the entire semester. I gave up instantly and didn't even consider studying for my exams.

Receiving my grades that semester was painful, and it sucked all the pride I possessed out of my system. The feeling in my chest was similar to the feeling of an ancient soldier getting a sharp sword pressed slowly through his chest, and being left to die on the battlefield. The difference here was I didn't feel any of the honor attributed to those bygone warriors whatsoever. I looked at my 0.8 GPA for the semester, with a 1.142 cumulative GPA and felt for the first time completely embarrassed and ashamed of myself. I was so out of it that I don't even remember how my mother reacted, or what she said.

I do remember, however, that she never, not once, put me down or made me feel like I was incapable of succeeding. It is amazing! After I messed up over and over again, my mother would continue to drill into my head that I was intelligent and could do anything I put my mind to. I knew at that point that no matter what happened in my life, my family would continue trying to motivate me. They would always love me unconditionally.

Chapter 11

I Have A Problem

The first step in solving a problem is admitting that you have one. I mentioned before that this was the first time I had felt ashamed of myself. It was also the first time I was able to admit to myself that I had a problem and it needed to be fixed. I had made up my mind that I would do whatever it took to get my life back on track. I spent a couple of weeks searching my mind for answers. I wanted to do something good, to redeem myself. I wanted to make my family proud. I just didn't have the slightest clue how to do that.

My heart told me that I wasn't ready to return to any type of school. I knew I didn't want to work someplace and just make minimum wage. I wanted to be successful. The question was how.

The answer came from the person I would have least expected, my stepfather, Mike. I say that Mike was the person I least expected my solutions from because after my mother remarried, I made a point not to listen to what he had to say. I loved to rebel and do the opposite of whatever he asked me to do. It had nothing to do with him as a person. The feelings came from deep inside of me, probably because I missed my real father.

I very rarely discussed anything with my stepfather. When we spoke, it would be about something he loved, like hunting, cars, his job, or golf. I still don't know the reason he chose to open up to me and reveal his past, but I'm glad he did. He told me about his high school days playing football, and chasing girls. Then he told me of his college days at East Carolina University, and all the partying he had done. It was a major shock for me to hear this type of disclosure from my stepfather. I couldn't believe my ears! All this time I was getting crap for the way I had acted in college, and here he was confessing that he made some of the same mistakes.

It was unbelievable, but good for me to hear. It gave me a sense of hope. You see, Mike did not do well during his first year of school, and had no idea of what he wanted to do with his life. He explained that he didn't want to waste his parents' money, so he enlisted in the Army and was shipped off to basic training. The Army taught him discipline and responsibility. I sat there listening to old boot camp stories about running though fields, shooting weapons, throwing grenades, and getting into shape. I liked the sound of all that and my interest increased by the minute. My stepfather also added that he thought it was a fun and easy way to make money. It was a persuasive move on his part. I don't know about you, but the idea of having fun while making money sounded mighty good to me.

I began thinking about joining the Army. I decided to call my father, who had been in the Air Force, to get his opinion. I didn't have to ask much about the Air Force before my father said, "it was the best days of my life, and I wish I had never gotten out." That was all I needed to hear in order for me to make a trip to the recruiting station to see what the Army was all about.

Chapter 12

My Solution—Army National Guard

When I arrived at the recruiting station I remember thinking *what in the world are you doing Skinner? The Army, for Pete's sake! Have you gone mad?*

I was still unsure about my decision until the recruiter began talking about paying for my college education. Instantly, light bulbs flickered on in my mind, illuminating a really great idea. This was my opportunity to make my family proud. I could join the military, pay for my own education through military benefits, and return to Radford. After basic training in the National Guard, you only have to do drill (which means Army stuff) once a month and two weeks out of the year; I would only have to work once a month, and my school would be paid for. I thought the idea was perfect. Before I left the office that day, I signed myself up for the Army National Guard and set a date for a physical and testing session.

Soon, I found myself sitting at an airport in Beckley, West Virginia. I was waiting to be shipped to Fort Benning, Georgia, where I would spend my whole summer wearing camouflage and being trained to kill as an infantryman.

I have to bluntly disagree with both my stepfather and my father. The Army was neither easy, nor the best time of my life. I admit that some of it was fun, but for the most part, I was miserable. In fact, I remember telling friends that it was by far the most miserable I had ever been.

I didn't mind the physical training, dressing in camouflage, saying "yes Drill Sergeant," "no Drill Sergeant," being bossed around, or even being constantly yelled at. I wasn't afraid or intimidated by any means. In that respect, getting into my fraternity was much harder.

The part that killed me was the downtime, those hours when we weren't busy doing Army things. Those were the times when your mind would wander and you would begin to miss the real world. You'd start to think about being able to come and go as you please, make telephone calls, watch TV, listen to the radio, go to the movies, hang out with friends, pick out your own outfit, and interact with girls. Most importantly, interact with girls. We weren't allowed any of these things during basic training.

During downtimes, I would observe guys writing letters to their families, friends, girlfriends, and wives. These men would just sit on the floor with a picture in their hand, staring, with tears slowly running down their face.

I dreaded the end of each day. I knew that as darkness fell, so would our spirits. Crawling into the bed at night felt good initially, because my body was totally exhausted, but the feeling did not last. There was something about the silence in the barracks at night that always gave me a sick feeling in my stomach. The air was thick with the sadness of sixty homesick, exhausted men from all over the United States. It was difficult to stay positive and motivated.

I had a difficult time making friends at boot camp, because most of the guys were so negative. After the first month, I noticed that one particular guy in my platoon stood out, Brad from Montana. He always had a smile on his face and seemed so content. He was friendly, sincere, and generous to everyone. He seemed too good to be true. Brad was the kind of guy you just wanted to choke, because he aggravated you by being so happy-go-lucky all the time. During his free time he would always keep to himself and read his Bible. I decided to study him, like a science experiment. I wanted to know his secret.

How does he stay so positive and confident? Could it be that Bible? I would ask myself. I watched him closely, waiting for him to break down like everyone else. Sadly, I sort of wanted him to break down. I wanted him to break down so badly that when he didn't, it frustrated me to the point that I couldn't take it anymore. I had to go talk to him and get an explanation.

One day after chow, I approached him. He was sitting up against a tree reading his Bible, smiling peacefully. Without a word of greeting, I sat down directly in front of him and stared.

"All right man, how do you do it?" I asked.

"Do what?" he responded, gently.

"How do you stay so peaceful and content throughout the day?" I was frustrated.

He put his Bible down for a second and looked me in the eyes. It felt like he was looking right through to my soul, as he quickly made his assessment of me. He asked, "Do you believe in God?"

"Yeah, yeah, of course. Doesn't everybody? Besides what does that have to do with it?"

He got this little grin on his face, like he was giving me a present and couldn't wait for me to open it.

"Come here, let me show you something," he said while pointing his finger to a place in his Bible. I scooted over beside him for a better view.

"Read this scripture," he said. His grin transformed into a full-fledged smile. That smile gave me comfort, but not nearly as much comfort as I felt while reading the scripture. It was plain and simple, yet so powerful.

"I can do all things through Christ who strengthens me."

I raised my head up slowly. A smile developed on my face as the words sunk into my heart. With a grin from ear to ear, Brad placed his hand on my shoulder, nodded, and said, "You see man, with Jesus as your Lord and Savior you can accomplish anything!"

He paused for a second, then as his eyes began to water he continued, "No matter where you are in life, no matter what the circumstances are, if you just put your faith in Jesus, he will provide you with 'The peace that surpasses all understanding.'"

At that moment, I put my head down and closed my eyes. I felt like a car had been lifted off of my chest. I experienced a feeling of contentment and peace like never before. The feeling was so beautiful and overwhelming; tears of joy began rolling down my cheeks. I lifted my head, now wearing the same big smile as Brad and extended my hand in gratitude. Brad reached out, meeting my hand with his and said, "Thank the Lord."

From that day on, during free time Brad and I would sit together. We shared the stories of our lives and read the Bible. I wrote home asking my parents to send me a Bible, which they did eagerly. I had figured out his, or should I say *His*, secret. The Lord offers love to all. I began to get my priorities straight, keeping my foot locker clean, hustling in and out of the barracks, and giving my all in everything that I did.

As boot camp dragged on and became more strenuous physically, I discovered that it was less strenuous mentally and emotionally. I continued to focus on my faith, which helped me maintain a positive attitude. No matter what twists and turns the day brought, I was mentally strong and able to feel content regardless of my situation.

Before I knew it, boot camp was over, and I was on an airplane heading home with my head held high. My confidence had been restored. I will never forget the feeling of pride and accomplishment I felt when I stepped off the airplane in full military uniform and saw my family looking at me through the glass of the terminal. I walked proudly, feeling like a new man, towards the terminal to reunite with them. When I turned the corner, my mom ran toward me and wrapped me in a tight hug. She told me how proud she was. I hugged the rest of my family and then gave my step-dad a quick jab in the arm to say thanks in a manly, nonchalant kind of way. The feeling of love and excitement they expressed to me was priceless. It felt as if they were sharing my feelings of accomplishment with me. I immediately began telling boot camp stories as we walked to the car and stuffed all my clothes and souvenirs in the back.

I took a moment of silence as we pulled away from the airport to reflect on the feelings that we had all just experienced. I turned my head to watch the terminal grow smaller as we drove away. At first, I felt a sense of sadness weighing me down inside because the moment had passed. It felt like Christmas morning when all the presents have been opened and you suddenly realize that Christmas is over for another year. The heavy feeling was lifted from my chest when my consciousness led me to think about Brad's smile, our discussions, and the Prince of Peace, Jesus Christ. I quickly turned around in my seat, regained the focus and composure I had learned. As my cheesy smile returned, I thought about the accomplishments still to come.

The sky's the limit, I repeated in my mind.

Chapter 13

One More Chance

My original plan upon returning was to live at home in Franklin, VA and attend Paul D. Camp Community College. PDCCC was less than five miles from my house. Enrolling seemed like the most logical thing to do in many regards. I could attend school, get my grades up in a less distracting environment, work part-time, and save money on rent and food. I signed up for classes, but my plan was too good to be true.

The weekend before school started, I had to return to Radford to pick up some of the stuff that I had left behind. Driving back into that little town made me smile. It was my home away from home. Wasting no time, I drove straight to my fraternity house to pay my respects and let the boys know I was in town. I turned onto the street and saw the old fraternity house that held so many of my memories, both good and bad. As usual, there were guys sitting on the porch and lounging in the yard. Drinking beer and listening to music out on the porch was a fraternity tradition. It was exactly like I remembered, and it felt like I never even left. When I pulled up in front of the house, I received a couple of blank stares. The guys didn't recognize me at first. You see, when I left for basic training, I had shoulder length hair. I also was about seventeen pounds skinnier, and wore raggedy clothes and hemp necklaces. Now I was clean cut, standing straight and tall, and in topnotch shape.

I walked on to the porch and said, "Hey fellows, I'm back!"

After a brief pause one of the guys yelled, "Skinner! Hey

man, you look great. But what's up with the bald head?" We all laughed, exchanged handshakes and hugs, and immediately started catching up with each other. Just like old times.

I should have sensed the first sign of trouble. They offered me a beer, and I accepted it. At the time, I felt confident and in control of my desires. Even though my friends teased and ragged on me for not continuing to drink, I finished my beer and left to gather up my stuff and return home.

I went over to another fraternity brother's apartment where I kept some things while I was at basic training. Seeing my friends and brothers was awesome. Their reaction was positive, and the familiar faces were welcoming.

As I packed my things into the truck, my mind started wandering.

Maybe I could come live here, and go to New River Community College.

Right at that moment, a friend came outside to persuade me to stay.

"Skinner, we have an open room in our apartment. Why don't you just stay here with us? Come on man, how could you just leave all of this?"

"Sorry man, I just can't do it," I said, but I wasn't very sure of myself. My friend quickly sensed the debate going on in my mind.

"Well, at least stay for the night. We are having a party here tonight!"

Although it was obvious to him I was trying to change my lifestyle, my old friend knew that I couldn't resist that offer. I knew that I shouldn't, but I relented. I nodded and agreed to stay, warning that I had to get up early and leave.

"Sure thing. You can use my alarm clock," my friend

concluded, triumphantly putting the cherry on top. I'd placed myself in a tempting situation. In less than an hour, I'd already had a beer and changed my original plans.

The night came, and with it came the party. I won't lie and say I didn't have a good time seeing all my old buddies. I did. In fact, I had a blast. I can tell you, however, that I maintained my composure and didn't go overboard with my drinking. As people piled into the apartment and I reunited with my friends, I kept wondering, *Can I really leave all of this?*

I tried to convince myself that I had grown up and was able to live in a college atmosphere and still keep my priorities in line. I made it through the party without giving in to temptation. I stood strong. I actually got to sleep at a decent hour, which made it easy to wake up bright and early the next morning. I got up and attempted to say goodbye to my friends, but they were passed out all over the place. I jumped in the truck, and headed home as planned.

On my way home, I replayed the previous night in my head. I was proud of myself, and my confidence was renewed. I had proved my ability to act maturely. I wanted to make my family proud. On the other hand, I couldn't get the thought of living with my friends and attending classes at New River Community College out of my mind. I wanted to live my own life and have fun. I didn't have many friends back home, and I knew it would be a lonely year.

By the end of my five-hour drive, I had decided to return to Radford and go to New River Community College. The only issue I faced was how to pay for it. I called my friend from my cell phone just before I got home and asked him how much he would charge me for rent. After I explained my money problems and living situation to him, we came to an agreement that I thought would work.

As I walked up to the house, my emotions changed faster

than a ride on a roller coaster. I knew my mom would disagree and not support my plans. I opened the front door silently, hoping to buy myself enough time to plan a strategy. I looked down the hallway and I saw my mother sitting at the kitchen table, alone in the dark. Her hands were gently folded together, prayer-like. I knew she was waiting for me. There would be no reprieve.

I walked down the hallway and into the kitchen to reveal my change of plans. Immediately after switching on a light, I noticed her eyes were moist from crying. Without saying a word, I sat down in the chair across from her. She looked into my eyes and I could tell that she knew what I was about to say.

I blurted out, "I can't do it Mom, I'm sorry! I can't stay here. You have to understand, I've got to return to Radford."

"I know son. I knew it as soon as you walked out that door yesterday and headed back to that place!" She looked like she was doing everything in her power to hold back tears.

"Mom, you have to believe me. I can do it this time! I have learned a lot from the Army. I am ready!" I explained how I had been able resist temptation the night before.

She sat and listened quietly, disappointment written all over her face. She finally spoke.

"I don't agree, but okay. You are an adult now, and capable of making your own decisions. But this time, Chris, you are on your own!"

It hurt more than anything to hear her words, but I understand why she had to say them. Her pain must have been greater than mine the night she acknowledged my right to make decisions. She was letting me follow my own path, and she was letting me walk alone into my own mistakes. She knew me better than I knew myself.

We left the table and went upstairs. My mom helped me pack my things and put them in the truck. Wasting no time, I hopped in the truck, waved goodbye, and headed back to Radford.

I was nervous about being on my own, supporting myself financially, and taking a full class load. The Army paid fifty percent of my tuition, and I received a check once a month for drill that helped me pay the remainder of my tuition and the cost of books. For spending money I got a part-time job as an assistant manager at a local deli. I made about six dollars an hour, plus tips if I delivered food.

Needless to say, I was pretty tight on money, but managed to get along. I usually worked five to six days a week, on seven-hour shifts. Luckily, my boss was pretty flexible and worked around my classes. It felt like all I did was work, study, eat, and sleep. It was a hectic schedule, but good for me because it kept me out of trouble. I was usually too busy or too tired to do much partying. Although it was hard, I felt good about my effort and myself. I had a sense of accomplishment and perseverance.

I had mostly morning classes, so I had to get up early and drive to school. New River Community College was about twenty-five miles away from Radford, but felt more like one hundred miles. Despite the grueling drive, I continued to wake up every morning and make it to class on time. The determination to succeed was boiling in my blood, making me stronger. This willpower was becoming more and more a part of my daily routine.

Attending class regularly, getting to know my professors, and completing all my class assignments were new experiences for me. I was amazed at how well it seemed to be working. It must seem like common sense to most of you to attend class and complete assignments, but I honestly didn't know how to be a student. I remember calling my mom after doing well on my first test.

"Mom, all the stuff from class and in the reading assignments was on the test. It was great."

She giggled and said sarcastically, "No way, isn't that amazing. Who would have thought the reading assignments and class discussions would be on the test?"

We both laughed. I realized how well I could have been doing all along, and, for the first time in my life, I started to enjoy learning. After doing my reading assignments, I was able to engage in class discussions, because I actually knew what the rest of the students were talking about. That was fun and exciting for me, because I loved getting involved and voicing my opinion. I started to enjoy taking quizzes and tests simply for the sake of competition. I enjoyed competing within myself to strive for excellence, and competing with classmates to see who could score the highest grades. I realized that there are many different ways for people to learn. In my case, because of my competitive attitude, I decided to treat school like a sport. Learning was a game.

With this new outlook on education, I was able to finish out the remainder of the semester successfully. I ended up with one A, two Bs, and one C, for an overall grade point average of 3.0. I always joke about that C, saying the only reason I got it was because the teacher did not like me. Honestly, the reason I received the C in the easiest class I was taking, a Health class, was that I took the work for granted and spent the majority of my time studying for the other courses. From this humbling lesson, I learned to always give one hundred percent effort in everything I do, regardless of how simple a situation may seem.

The most exciting part about my achievement was that I was now eligible to reapply to Radford University. I had completed a year of suspension and also had taken a full load of classes, meeting the minimum requirement of a 3.0 GPA. I was so excited on the day I received my grades that I drove immediately to Radford University's registrar's office and picked up an application for readmission. As soon as I got home, I began filling out all the necessary forms. I remember my hand was shaking because I was so nervous about the possibility of not being reaccepted. I analyzed everything that I had been through to get to this point. I began contemplating whether it was worth it, if I happened to be turned down. I paused for a few minutes, and said a prayer asking God to humble me and to help me think optimistically. I opened my eyes, filled out the rest of the application, sealed it in an envelope with a quick lick, and took it straight back to the registrar's office.

Feeling a bit anxious, I asked the lady at the desk, "Would you happen to know when I will get an answer back?"

"I'm sorry, sir. I don't know exactly how fast they turn these things around," she said routinely. She gets those types of questions all the time.

I left the office feeling less anxious, and somewhat optimistic. I liked the way she said "turn these things around." I mean, that sounds pretty optimistic. I felt like she was telling me that they would be letting me know soon of my reacceptance. My reacceptance at Radford University wasn't so doubtful, after all. When I got accepted, it would be a sign of turning things around in my life.

I went home that day and tried to remain humble and realistic. I resumed my everyday life and tried not to think about Radford University and readmission. I did a pretty good job at it too, if you don't count all the times I checked my mailbox. I would check the mailbox twice a day, once in the morning when I got up, and then again late at night when I got home from work. I know it was silly, especially since the mailman only comes once a day, but I just couldn't wait for the answer. I hoped that I would once again experience that ever so sweet feeling of accomplishment.

I got the letter after two and a half weeks, exactly eighteen days. I passed the mailman on my way to work just as he was putting mail in our slots. My initial thought was to go on to work and check my mail when I get home. I was running late and I had already checked the mail once that day. I was already in my truck with the engine running when I saw the mailman slip a couple of envelopes in my slot. I got a funny feeling that today was the day. Without hesitation, I jumped out of my truck and began walking toward the mailbox. I was still trying to stay humble and to control my excitement. My effort apparently wasn't working too well. I was in such a hurry that I had locked my keys in the truck. The engine was still running. I opened my mailbox and began sorting through the mail.

At first, I was disappointed. I sifted through the stack of letters, which appeared to be all junk mail. At the end of the pile there it was—the second to last envelope. I paused for just an instant and said one last prayer before ripping the envelope open and unfolding the letter which held the answers to my future. I almost cried when I read the first word, "Congratulations," and then laughed with joy as I finished the rest of my acceptance letter. I thanked God for my perseverance, then immediately called my family and shared the great news. I felt great. I was on the way to achieving my goal of graduating from Radford University with a four-year degree.

After gloating over my success, I called the police. I needed their help to get back into my truck. I arrived at work about forty-five minutes late. I got a little steam from my boss, but at that point I felt unstoppable. I was so proud of myself that day; there wasn't much that would have been able to rain on my parade.

The next day I was so excited that I got up early and returned to the registrar's office. I signed up for Summer Session courses starting on June 25, which was just a couple of weeks away. I was officially back on track and feeling better than ever. Everything was falling into place just the way I wanted. I was feeling good. In fact, I was feeling on top of the world.

In sports, when a team is winning and on top, what happens? What usually happens is the last place team sneaks up and upsets them, because a team on top will invariably let their guard down. They just start thinking they are unbeatable, and that breaks down their defenses. This is exactly what happened to me. I let my guard down, and I started backsliding. The semester was over and I was on break until the beginning of Summer Session. My friends starting calling me to come on out and party.

They said, "You've worked hard this semester, Skinner. You hardly went out at all. You got the grades, proved to everyone that you can do it and now you've made it back into Radford University. You deserve a little time for yourself and your bros."

I thought, *What can letting off a little steam hurt?*

So I started going out. The first night, I was in control. I handled myself. That gave me the justification to do it again. Every night I went out, I lost a little more control. Finally, I was back in the habit of partying all night, then sleeping it off until time to get up and go to work. I told myself that this was just until the break was over. I could get things under control any time I needed.

Since then, I've learned to say, "If you can't resist temptation, then don't put yourself in a position to be tempted." The smart thing to do when you can't handle temptation is to avoid it. I hadn't learned that yet. Nor had I admitted to myself that I really did have a serious problem with alcohol. I fell back into my old pattern of behavior in less than a week's time.

Chapter 14

A Day To Remember

June 10, 2000 is a day that I will remember until the day I die. It is the day that I came face to face with my own frailty, and with the precious value of life.

When I awoke on June 10, 2000, I had no idea what the day had in store. It was just another typical day for a typical frat boy. I had no idea that the decisions I would make that day would change my life irreversibly. For twenty years, I had been preparing to live life on my own. There was never a question that I would be an independent man.

If someone told me that day that I would forever be dependent on others for my existence, I wouldn't have believed them. If they told me I would never walk, or feel my body again, I would have laughed in their face and called them crazy.

The day started like most of my days. I woke up with a hangover from partying too much the night before. The door opened and my little brother in the fraternity, Adam, walked in.

"Hey Skinner are you ready to go?"

I opened my eyes and groaned. Streams of sunlight filtered into my bedroom. It was a nightmare; I had been out all night partying and just made it to bed three hours before.

"I'm not going. Go away," I moaned. I covered my face with the nearest pillow to shield my eyes from the invasive sunlight. Adam wouldn't take no for an answer.

"Skinner you've got to go! It's Scott's wedding. We have been planning this!"

I didn't say a word. I hoped he would get the picture—I wasn't interested in going anywhere but back to sleep in my warm bed. I continued in my silence until I heard the door slam shut and the coast was clear. I then took the pillow from my face and began talking to myself out loud.

"Why did you go out all night when you knew you had to get up early and go to the wedding? You idiot, when will you learn?" I lectured myself.

"You know if you don't go, you will feel terrible about it later," I reasoned, "You already feel terrible now. There is no need to set yourself up to feel terrible twice in one day."

Normally, I would have turned over and gone back to sleep until late afternoon. Today was different because two of my best friends were getting married and I felt they expected me to be there. I made the decision to attend. Reluctantly, I rolled out of bed and onto my feet, letting out a miserable frustrated sigh. As I walked to the bathroom, I tried to think of a good excuse to turn around and go back to bed. I complained about how terrible I felt the entire time. I didn't know it would be the last time I would ever get out of bed on my own.

I jumped into the shower and let the cold water run over my body and bring me to full consciousness. After I dried off, I dressed in my best clean clothes and stood in front of the mirror to consider my reflection. I had a muscular build now, thanks to the Army.

Skinner, you are going to break some hearts tonight, I thought. I was right, in a prophetic way.

I hurried out the door, got into my little green pickup truck, and drove over to Adam's house. Without knocking (we never knocked), I barged through the front door and yelled, "Get in the truck you little rat." He came around the corner with a big smile on his face, like a little kid on Christmas Day. He walked right past me and got into the truck.

After a two-hour drive up I-81, we arrived in Harrisonburg, Virginia, for the wedding. The day seemed so normal, so ordinary. The only exceptional detail about the day, in fact, was the wedding itself.

The wedding was beautiful. It was held in a church filled with family and friends, all dressed up in their best attire. I hardly recognized some of my fraternity brothers. My friends, Scott and Kelly, looked so happy together.

I thought to myself, *Life is a beautiful adventure. It is so awesome to see two people in love.*

It was a comfortable moment. I sat with a contented smile on my face, pleased with the decision that I made to attend. I got caught up in the emotions of the moment and began daydreaming of my future life, wife and kids. Maybe we would play baseball together at the park. My mind wandered happily.

I woke from my daydream when the wedding ended and everyone was filing out of the church. Adam and I made our way to the truck. We both had to work the next morning at ten o'clock. We had agreed to skip the reception and leave immediately. A friend's car pulled up in front of us. He rolled down his window, and stuck his head out.

"Skinner, are you going to the reception?" he asked. "There are hot air balloons, food, live music, kegs of beer and, of course, ladies! You've got to come and check it out."

Adam and I looked at each other and shrugged our shoulders. It was another turning point for the day, another moment of decision. We decided it wouldn't hurt to eat a little wedding cake before we left.

I said, "We could go for a little while, and then head back"

Adam agreed, "Sure, we can check it out. We just won't drink anything. Right, Skinner?"

"That's right my man!" I said. But thoughts of partying started sneaking into my mind.

We followed the rest of the crew down the country back roads to the reception. These were the kind of roads that are so narrow that you say to yourself, "Man, I hope no one comes around these curves at the same time I do. There can't possibly be enough room for both of us." The windows were down and I could feel the hot, humid wind against my face. Adam and I glanced at each other every so often and smiled.

The reception was everything that was promised and then some. It was held in a giant field of bright green grass. Next to the field was a large pond, with little white-tailed ducks swimming around it in circles. There were hot air balloons hovering as high as a five-story building, glowing in a bright multicolor blaze. They looked like rainbows—minus the pot of gold. If you stood underneath them they blocked the sky. There were white, circus sized canopy tents sheltering lines of tables. Some tables were meant for people to sit, while others were covered with an unlimited assortment of food. I felt just like a Pilgrim on Thanksgiving.

I was glad we decided to attend the reception, after all. This was a grand celebration. There was loud music playing with several people were already dancing, many of whom were gorgeous young women dressed in evening dresses.

Yesss, I thought to myself.

Just when I thought it couldn't get any better, my eyes suddenly locked in on the ice-cold kegs of beer and boxes of wine sitting so beautifully at the end of the serving line. Immediately, my mouth dropped and I began to salivate. Adam knew me too well. He knew that I would make the decision to drink. He put his hand in the air as if to say "hand them over, Skinner!" With absolutely no hesitation, I tossed him the keys to my truck and winked.

"Might as well have one or two," I said, "Besides, we shouldn't let all that beer go to waste."

I made a dash for the beer, anticipating that feeling of gratification that comes with the first sip. There was a crowd around the end of the serving line, blocking my way to the liquid satisfaction. After a few moments of boxing people out, and squeezing my empty cup through the gaps, my quest was nearly complete.

I filled my cup to the top slowly, making sure I maintained a precise angle so that the beer would have less foam. I brought the cold cup to my mouth, The Holy Grail. The heavenly froth spilled slowly down the side. Finally, I had arrived at the moment I had been waiting for. This was the beginning of another delightful liaison between beer and my stomach. As the first sip trickled down my throat and into my stomach, I reminisced about the good times beer and I have shared. My mind drifted into a delighted daze, alcohol la-la land, if you will. The bottom of the cup abruptly interrupted my state of bliss.

Man, that was great, I will just have to have another, I thought. *It's only right.*

I filled my cup back to the brim and dove back into the bliss. Soon I was chugging beer like a lost man in a desert, like I hadn't had a drink of anything for days and had just stumbled upon a pond of crystal clear water. Needless to say, one thing led to another. Before long, I was drunk.

Suddenly, Adam nudged me.

"We have to go Skinner," he advised. "I've got to get back and get some sleep. I can't be late for work tomorrow."

Remembering our agreement, I put my head down and followed Adam to the truck. I wished I could come up with a good reason to stick around, but could think of no angle that would persuade him to stay. I wanted him to call in sick, but he refused. His decision was no fun, but it was one I could respect. He had self-control, and didn't let the party call the shots for him.

While we were pulling away, we were slowed by a congestion of cars. Of course, it seemed that everyone was trying to leave at the same time. We were sitting dead still when a couple of friends knocked on my window. I rolled down my window to say goodbye.

"Are you leaving already? The party is just getting started," they coaxed.

"I don't want to leave," I said, sensing a window of opportunity. "Adam has to work in the morning."

"We are all going back to Radford tomorrow morning. You can catch a ride with us if you want," they said.

They didn't have to make the offer twice. I decided to stay. I looked at Adam, and smiled.

"Drive safely," I told him. "And don't wreck my truck," I added. I knew my parents would kill me if they knew I was letting him drive it in the first place.

I hopped out of the truck, slammed the door behind me, and followed the crowd back to the Promised Land. We continued to have a blast, laughing, drinking, and dancing. Later came wrestling (I know, what a bunch of meatheads we were), scoping out girls, playing the hokey-poky, and trying to catch the garter that was pulled off the beautiful bride.

It was all fun and games while the party lasted. Then all of a sudden the music stopped, the beer was gone, the girls all left, and the excitement was over. There were seven guys, including me, left alone in the field. We looked around, bewildered, like a bunch of lost puppies. It was time for us to go, but we had no idea where.

All of us were drunk. We had no way to get to our hotels, except to drive. I decided to ride with drunk drivers. Unfortunately, it wasn't the last time that night I would make such a foolish choice. We piled into cars and went on our way. We then decided we were not finished throwing down, so we stopped at a little gas station and bought a couple of cases of beer. I guess we felt like we hadn't killed enough brain cells that night.

We arrived at the hotel late that evening, around midnight. We sat around and challenged each other to drink more, to drink faster. Soon, the people who rented the hotel rooms were ready for bed. We called them wimps. They were party-poopers, but I'd say they where pretty doggone smart.

One of the guys, still willing to party, was local.

"I live just a few miles away. We can all go there and party as long as we want," he said.

It's just a few miles. I thought. *We used to run that far in high school. We're drunk, but not that drunk. Besides I've driven drunk way farther than that before and nothing ever happened to me.*

My friends and I are a perfect example of how dumb people can be sometimes. We made a terrible decision, despite our knowledge of the dangerous consequences. The rationalization people will give themselves for doing something they shouldn't is astounding (not to mention frightening). We piled into the cars again, even drunker than before.

You're probably saying to yourself, "enough is enough, buddy. Just go to sleep." Trust me, you're right. I made bad choice after bad choice, and it was heading nowhere good. I will always be very frustrated when I think back about my decisions that night.

I hopped in the back seat of a friend's Explorer. Before we pulled away, another friend of ours pulled in beside us. Out of the corner of my eye, I saw his big, black Blazer. It was an older brother in the fraternity—my "Grand" big brother. We had known each other for a few years, and I felt pretty comfortable around him.

Then it happened. In my memories, I still see every movement he made. He sat alone, casually listening to music. One hand rested on the steering wheel, and the other hand dangled out the window. At six foot, six inches, and pushing two hundred and fifty pounds, he was a pretty solid guy. He reached over slowly, turned his radio down, and leaned toward our car.

"Hey Skinner," he said, "come get in the car with me. You can ride shotgun."

"Oh, yeah! SHOTGUN!" I said, jokingly. "Let me out guys."

As I jumped out of the car, I slapped the back of one guy's head. I laughed hysterically, and he jumped out of the Explorer and chased me around our friend's Blazer a few times. I realized we weren't going anywhere until he caught me, so I stopped. He grabbed me and gave me a quick jab in the arm, leaving a stinging Charlie horse. Then he jumped back in his car, and I took shotgun position in the Blazer.

After exchanging a handshake, we followed the rest of the posse down the pitch-black, winding country roads. I wondered if anyone would be out driving on these roads this late at night. Then I noticed two beer cans in the drink holders. One beer was open, and one was still closed. I grabbed my seat belt, and fastened it tight.

For a split-second, I questioned whether I should be riding in a vehicle with any of these guys. Twenty years before, almost to the month, a drunk driver had killed my aunt on her way home from a wedding reception. As you can imagine, I had been warned often not to ride with anyone who had been drinking. After examining my friend's composure, eyes, size, and weight, I decided we would be okay.

He doesn't look drunk. Shoot, it must take a truckload of alcohol to really affect that big fella.

There were six cars in our caravan, and we were the last of the pack. "Crash into Me," by Dave Matthews Band, started to play on the CD player. I reached down and cranked the volume so high that I'm surprised the windows didn't shatter. My friend and I jammed down the road playing air guitars, lip synching, dancing to the music, and having the time of our lives.

I decided to throw a dip of chewing tobacco in before we got to the party, but I realized we would be at the house in just a few minutes. I needed time to dip, spit, and clean out my mouth before we got there, so I wouldn't gross out all the ladies. I had gotten addicted to the nasty stuff when I pledged the fraternity. I grabbed my blue can of Skoal Mint and threw a wad of tobacco under my bottom lip.

Suddenly, I realized that I didn't have anything to spit in. I looked all around the car and couldn't find anything, except for the open beer can. Even though I considered myself a pro at dipping, I always had trouble spitting into a 12-ounce can. The hole has a weird shape, and if I put my mouth around it, I'd cut my lips on the razor sharp aluminum. My friends who were "true dippers" always made fun of me. I shouted to my friend over the music.

"There's nothing to spit in."

I was starting to panic. I didn't want to swallow the juice. I had done that once before when I was a rookie. It had made me sick for days.

My friend yelled back at me and gestured outside.

"Spit out the window; just don't spit on my car!"

I then made the worst of my bad decisions. I reached down and took my seat belt off. This would enable me to lean out the window, so my spit would clear the car. I leaned out to spit several times, then decided to take my dip out once and for all. It always took me a few minutes to flush the tobacco pieces out of my mouth, and I wanted to give myself ample time to freshen up. We were one curve and seven hundred yards away from the house.

We were drunk, listening to loud music, doing forty-five miles per hour. The side of the road was spread with loose gravel. I leaned out the window as we went around the curve. The curve was sharp.

My friend lost control of the vehicle.

I remember a loud screeching noise and the feeling of the car being lifted off the ground.

Chapter 15

The Accident

We fishtailed and the car flipped two and a half times. I was catapulted from the passenger seat, out the window, and through the air. I hit the ditch, my right shoulder leading the way. I can still hear the screeching of the tires, the sound of several thousand pounds of metal bouncing down the road and into the ditch. The impact for me was hard and sudden.

Instantly, my right shoulder blade (scapula) broke completely in half. The cochlea in my right ear was shattered, leaving me deaf on that side. My neck was broken at the C5–C6 vertebrae, injuring my spinal cord from C1 to C7. This left me paralyzed from my shoulders down, which the doctors say is for life.

I remember lying in the ditch motionless, gasping for air like a fish out of water, trying to figure out what the heck just happened. I turned my eyes to the right and saw the Blazer, mangled and upside down about twenty feet away from me. I was lucky that it hadn't rolled over me. The wheels were still spinning. The headlights were still shining. I heard the stereo still playing "Crash into Me." That song gives me chills to this day.

Then I noticed something moving in the Blazer. I saw my friend drag himself out of the vehicle with his elbows. He shook his head and felt his body to make sure he was still in one piece. When he got himself together, it was like a light switched on and he remembered that I'd been in the car with him. He looked in the car, and then toward the ditch. He finally made eye contact with me. It was the most frightening eye contact I have ever had in my life.

There was a slight pause. He was soaking in the severity of the situation. He was probably thinking to himself, *This is not happening. This can't be real.* I know that's what I was thinking.

He came closer. My friend looked dazed, almost like he was in shock. He knelt on one knee beside me and wiped blood away from my mouth.

"Skinner, come on man stay with me." His voice was fearful.

My eyes rolled to the back of my head; I couldn't focus. My vision faded in and out like a video camera.

He touched the side of my face gently and I regained focus for a minute. I whispered, "Take the dip out of my mouth." I was choking on something and didn't know whether it was saliva or blood.

The cars in front of us apparently realized we were not following them anymore. The crew came looking for us. I saw my friends run up to us, then stop dead in their tracks. The looks on their faces were like none I have ever seen. They stood above me speechless, with their mouths gaping wide open. I heard a couple of girls crying in the background. Some were singing songs, to keep themselves calm.

I couldn't feel anything, and I was terrified. I remember looking down and seeing my body lying in an awkward position, unable to move. Another friend of mine reached down and began tickling my feet.

"Can you feel this, Skinner?" He asked, concerned. He sounded as though he didn't know if he wanted to hear the answer.

"I'm…I'm paralyzed. I'm paralyzed. I can't feel anything."

I moaned. Tears began to roll down my face. I had never met any paralyzed people in my entire life. I didn't know what it really entailed. I knew it had just happened to me.

"No, you're not paralyzed Skinner," my friends tried to reassure me. "You're just in shock," they repeated over and over again. They were so afraid. They were trying to comfort me, but they were comforting themselves as well.

It was getting harder and harder to breathe. My neck was swelling, and it was beginning to close my air passage. For the first time in my life, I thought that I was going to die. I saw images of my family crying at my funeral. My mother was hysterical, her body thrown upon my casket, bear-hugging it with all her might. It was difficult to stay calm. I lay there and concentrated on my breathing. I forced myself to take short, shallow breaths.

I noticed the sky. It was perfectly clear and there were millions of beautiful, bright stars looking down on me. I gritted my teeth and thought to myself, *God, this can't be it! There is still so much to experience in life. Help me be strong and hang on! Help me keep my eyes open!*

I lay in that position for at least twenty minutes. Finally, I saw small blinking lights in the distance. They advanced down the road, toward me. As the lights got brighter and brighter, I heard the siren grow louder. Finally, I could see the white, box shaped ambulance. I noted the gigantic orange stripe down its side with blue letters that read "Emergency." Just before the ambulance came to a complete stop, I saw three strangers jump out, like Marines on a mission to save the world. They ran toward me at full speed.

They approached me looking like they had, unfortunately, dealt with this type of situation before. They all assumed their positions, one at my feet, one at my midsection, and one hovering over my head with a flashlight pointed directly in my eyes.

"What is your name? How old are you? Do you know what happened?" They asked several general questions as they surveyed my situation.

I remember moving my mouth in an attempt to answer, but I couldn't find the breath or the strength. I felt myself letting go, surrendering to exhaustion, and giving my fate to three strangers in dark blue pants, white shirts, and little EMT badges. I saw the backs of my eyelids as I fell deeply into unconsciousness. It was the world where I would remain for the next thirteen days.

While I slept, the EMTs continued doing their job, fighting to keep me alive until they could get me to the nearest hospital. After they loaded me into the ambulance and started to shut the doors, one of my friends, Tate, jumped into the ambulance and stayed by my side the whole time. He did not want me to be alone. Still tickling my feet and rubbing my legs, he encouraged me to stay strong. Although I have no memory of that ambulance ride, Tate told me that my eyes were open and I was attempting to communicate. With the sirens blasting and the lights flashing, the ambulance driver navigated as fast as possible down and around the pitch-black country roads toward Rockingham Memorial Hospital.

Upon our arrival at the hospital, the ambulance doors were torn open and I was dashed straight through the emergency room directly to a treatment room. Immediately a doctor came running in to evaluate my situation. After a quick x-ray, he found that my neck was broken and my spinal cord had been severed. He then knew that he wasn't equipped to handle injuries of this magnitude. Not more than fifteen minutes after arriving at Rockingham Memorial, they called for Pegasus, a medical transport helicopter. It would pick me up and fly me to the University of Virginia Medical Center in Charlottesville, Virginia. There, they would have the expertise, the staff, and the equipment to treat my injury.

As I was being loaded onto the helicopter, Tate was told he would not be allowed to go any further with me. He told me that watching me being wheeled away from him, strapped to a stretcher with needles and tubes all over my body, would haunt his dreams for the rest of his life. I am so thankful he was with me up to that point. In my heart, I know that hearing his voice and words of encouragement during those first few critical hours kept me alive.

I was flown to UVA Medical Center. A team of trauma doctors evaluated for themselves the severity of my injuries, and began taking action in order of medical importance.

Meanwhile, at their home in Smithfield, VA, my mother and stepfather were comfortably asleep in their king sized bed. Their phone rang at around 3:00 A.M.

I have no memory of the events that occurred over the next several days.

Chapter 16

From The Journal Of Jeanne Hinson

Sunday, June 11, 2000—A Mother's Worst Nightmare

I woke to the ringing of a telephone. This didn't instantly alarm me. Since the boys had been away at college, they often made late phone calls home without realizing what time it was. I glanced at the clock while I was picking up the receiver and noticed that it was 3:00 A.M. I felt a quick moment of apprehension because of the very late hour. A police dispatcher identified himself and asked me if I was the mother of Christopher Skinner. Instantly, I jumped out of the bed and stood at attention. My apprehension went straight to panic level. My mind started racing with suppositions.

A moment passed before I focused on the voice telling me that Chris had been in a car accident and was seriously injured. "That means he's alive!" I thought. I pulled my focus back to the dispatcher, who was telling me that the emergency room doctor needed to contact me. He instructed me to wait by the phone for his call. I started pacing back and forth, holding the phone to my chest and saying a quick prayer for help with this situation. My husband, Mike, realizing something was seriously wrong, got out of bed and came to me. He put his hands on my shoulders trying to get me to stop pacing while at the same time asking me, "What's wrong?" I was trying to hold myself together and was unable to respond to him. I was afraid that if I spoke, I might lose what little control I still had over my emotions.

Moments later the phone rang again and I answered on the first ring. The emergency room doctor told me his name and the hospital that he was calling from. He told me that Chris had been in a car accident and was severely injured. He told me that he was unable to handle the situation, and was sending Chris by helicopter to UVA Medical Center where he could receive the best treatment. He told me that I needed to get there quickly. My adrenalin kicked into gear and I told my husband to get ready because we had to leave.

I woke Tammy, Chris' sister, and told her about the accident and that I was leaving immediately. She was a high school senior, and it was graduation week. There were many special activities planned and I hated for her to miss any of them. I told her that she could go with us or stay home and go to school. She chose to go with us and asked if she should call her dad, also Chris' father. I told her to get ready and I'd call him, which I soon did. We quickly packed a few things and were en route to Charlottesville, VA by 3:30 A.M.

The ride to Charlottesville was surreal. We left in darkness with moonlight and starlight illuminating the countryside. The roads were nearly deserted and we went for hours without seeing other travelers. We didn't sleep, nor did we speak. We were all dealing with the news and processing our thoughts and feelings. We arrived at the hospital at 6:00 A.M and were met in the hallway by Wayne, the kid's dad. He said he had just arrived also, and told me that they needed me to go and do paperwork since Chris was on our insurance. Mike and I went to the business office as instructed. As we left, I watched Tammy walking toward the waiting room with her dad by her side. I wanted to put my arms around her and hold her close. I needed to feel my children close to me.

We had just taken our seats in the business office when an emergency room nurse ran in and shouted "Come quickly! We're taking your son to surgery."

Mike and I ran, following her to a boy with bleached yellow hair lying on a stretcher in front of an elevator. I stopped short and said, "That's not my son! That's not Chris!"

At the same time, the young man on the gurney said, "That's not my mother!" Then I saw the fear and disappointment in his eyes.

I looked at him and said, "I'm sorry." I wanted to hug him and tell him not to worry. His mother would be there soon. But they pushed him in the elevator and the doors closed as we stood there watching. I still remember his eyes. He was trying so hard to be a man and be strong.

Mike put his arm around me and steered me through the emergency room and back to the business office to finish the paperwork. We sat at the desk of the admissions clerk, while she asked us the required questions and typed our answers into her computer system. As we sat there, other clerks arriving for the day shift kept walking in and out, talking with her while we were sitting there. She chatted with them reporting how horrible the night had been.

"It has been unbelievable around here. We had several major traumas and eight deaths. All young people…all car accidents…all involving alcohol."

Well, that's all I needed to hear. I wanted to see Chris and I wanted to see him now. I asked the lady to get someone to take me to him. She called back to the ER and no one could tell me where Chris was or anything about his condition. She told us to have a seat in the waiting room and someone would come out and talk to us as soon as possible.

We finished the paperwork and joined Tammy and Wayne in the waiting room. We sat two more hours without hearing anything. We constantly checked with the woman at the information desk, asking if anyone could tell us anything. She said that someone would come out and talk with us as soon as possible. I kept praying that they had not mixed up the boys again and that my Chris was one of the fatalities. It was the longest two hours I have ever spent. It was sheer agony. Then someone over the intercom said, "Would the family of Chris Skinner assemble in the family conference room?"

He's dead, I thought as I slowly walked into the conference room. *We've been waiting all this time and he didn't make it and…I didn't get to talk to him.*

We sat and waited another eternity. Finally, a nurse with a sweet smile walked in removing a surgical cap from her head and looking very tired. She did a quick survey of the room and came and sat down beside me.

She took my hand in hers and said, "I've been with Chris since he arrived. I'm sorry that I didn't come out to talk with you, but I couldn't leave Chris. We've been working all this time to get him stable." She asked everyone to introduce themselves to her. Then she gave us the news about his situation.

She told us that he was in very critical condition. He had broken his neck and had a spinal cord injury. They had stabilized his neck by drilling holes in his head to hold a metal halo. Weights were suspended from the halo to traction his neck, pulling the vertebra back in position. She said he was paralyzed from the shoulders down. He had a ventilator breathing for him. He was being given steroids to keep the swelling to a minimum and prevent any more spinal cord damage. She said that he would need surgery when and if he became stable enough. She said he was young, strong, and in good health, but it would be 24–48 hours before we would know anything for sure. She asked if we had any questions.

I asked, "After the surgery, how long will it be before he gets better?"

She looked at me with such compassion as she said, "Honey, I'm sorry. He will never be the same again. With the type of injury Chris has, there is very little we can do. His paralysis is permanent."

I said quickly, "No one can know that for sure. Chris' condition is in God's hands."

She patted my hand again and said, "You're absolutely right and you keep believing that. Now let me take you to Chris."

She took us upstairs to the Neurological Intensive Care Unit and explained the procedure for getting admittance into the unit. "You have to push a button and ask permission to see the patient. Then you have to wash your hands with antibacterial gel that you get from the dispenser on the wall. Only two can visit at any time and he is supposed to have only ten minutes of visitation every hour, but they will usually allow more if the patient remains calm."

Then she said, "Okay, who's going first?" Wayne and Tammy said they would wait, so Mike and I went first.

The nurse pushed the button, asked for admittance and the huge doors swung open. As we walked through the doors I felt as if I was being strangled. I realized I was holding my breath and forced myself to take air into my lungs.

She had wanted to prepare us for seeing him as much as she could, but it was still a huge shock. My gaze swept around the room, taking in all the equipment, and then focused back on Chris. He was lying motionless on the bed with his eyes open staring at the ceiling. When he saw me, tears began streaming down his face. His expression showed the fear he was feeling. I approached the bed and stopped for a second to find a safe place that I could touch Chris. He had so many tubes and wires everywhere that I couldn't even hug him to comfort him. So, I put my hands on his shoulders and began rubbing them. Without realizing it, I did the right thing. He had no feeling anywhere else.

"Chris, it's Mom. I'm here now."

One of the many tubes, wires and machines that he was connected to was a ventilator and it was breathing for him. The ventilator was connected to a tube inserted in his mouth and down his throat. The machine made clicking sounds when it breathed for him and alarm noises when he got choked up—which he did when he saw us. The machine made an alarm sound and his eyes filled with terror. The alarm noises frightened him. The nurse told us that when he cries, he chokes and it messes up the rhythm of the machine. When it loses rhythm, it sounds an alarm.

I explained to Chris that a machine was breathing for him for now and they were trying to get him ready to go to surgery. As soon as he was able to have the surgery, things would get better. But right now, please be calm. I was there and I would not leave him. I kept rubbing his shoulders and his upper arm. I noticed how hot his skin felt, and then I realized that the room was freezing cold and he was lying there with absolutely nothing on except a towel placed over his private parts.

He had two tubes inserted through his nose that were attached to a pump that was beside his bed. One delivered liquid nourishment into his stomach and the other removed stomach acid and pumped it out to a receptacle sitting by the bed. The nurses checked it often, emptied it when necessary, and kept the reservoir filled with the liquid nourishment. Chris hated the tubes, and kept wiggling his nose.

Mike stood on the other side of the bed. He asked Chris if he remembered being in a car accident. Chris tried to speak and again the machine started alarming. Realizing that he shouldn't try to speak, Mike told him to blink his eyes—one blink for yes, two blinks for no and that we would only ask yes or no questions. We told him we loved him. We said that he was going to be okay, but in our hearts, we didn't know if that was true. We had yet to speak to a doctor.

Remembering that Tammy and Wayne were waiting to see Chris, we told Chris that we were going out so they could come in. His eyes registered alarm. I realized that he didn't want me to go.

I said, "Chris, I'll be here with you until you are better. I'm not going to leave you. They will only allow two people to visit you at a time so I have to go outside to the waiting room now and let *your father and Tammy come in to visit you. They are worried about you, too. I will be just outside and I'll be back as soon as they get a chance to say hello. Understand?"*

He blinked twice—"NO," with tears running down his cheeks.

Mike said, "you stay here and I'll go get them." So I waited with Chris, rubbing the tears off his face and kissing his forehead.

Tammy and Wayne came into the room and tried to mask their shock at seeing Chris in this shape. They apprehensively approached the bed and looked to find a place to touch him. I told them to rub his head or shoulders so he can feel them. They assured him that they loved him. Again, Chris was overcome with emotion and began to choke up, setting off the alarm on his machine. A nurse came rushing in and Tammy and Wayne stood back to allow her access.

She was so business-like as she said, "One of you will have to leave. Two visitors only." She punched buttons on the various machines, taking readings, and made entries to the computer that was attached to all of them.

I started to leave, but Chris looked at me and blinked twice —"NO."

Wayne patted him on the head and said, "I understand buddy. She's your mother." He said he would go and be back later.

Tammy said, "No, Dad. You stay and I'll go." She turned with tears in her eyes and practically ran out of the room. The nurse left the room, leaving us standing on either side of his bed, rubbing his head and shoulders and telling him things would be all right. The medication they gave him finally kicked in and Chris fell into a deep sleep.

We took turns sitting by his bed, constantly touching him so that he would remain calm and know that we were there. His body was blazing hot, but we were freezing in that cold room. His body was in shock. It was in a fight for his life.

We all took turns making phone calls. Mike made most of them for us, because I couldn't talk without crying. I didn't want to look like I had been crying when I was with Chris. The only one I called was Patrick. I wanted to be the one to tell him about his brother. I put it off as long as I could, because I wanted to have more information to give him. It was exam week for him and I wanted him to be able to concentrate on his studies and then he would have a three-week break. When I heard his voice on the phone, I broke down.

"Patrick, this is Mom. Chris has been in a car accident and we're at the hospital. Patrick, your brother is paralyzed. I'm so sorry to have to tell you this over the phone." Patrick started to cry.

"Mom, I have to come. Mom, I need to be there with you. I need to see my brother." I reminded him about exams. I told him to try to hang in there until he finished exams before he came. He said he didn't know how he was going to concentrate. I told him to do the best he could. Chris was sleeping and we were waiting for surgery. We hadn't talked to a doctor yet, but would call him when we had further information.

Later that evening, we insisted that a doctor be found to talk to us about Chris' situation. Finally, on Sunday evening at about 6:00 P.M., a resident doctor on the trauma team came to the waiting room and sat down with us to talk. Right there, in the middle of a huge waiting room filled with other strangers, he matter-of-factly explained the situation. He told us that Chris had broken his neck at C5–C6, with C5 being displaced 100%, which severed his spinal cord. He said the damage was extensive, running from C1 to C7. He said there was no way to tell right now, but most likely Chris would never walk again, never have use of his arms, and might never be able to breathe on his own. He drew a picture of the injury on a scrap of paper and said it was one of the five worst injuries they had ever seen in this hospital. He said Chris would need surgery to stabilize his neck as soon as he was able to handle the surgery. He said the injury was permanent, and except for the surgery, there wasn't anything else they could do.

I looked at him and said, "No! That can't be true. You have to be able to fix this. You have to be able to make him better." I finally broke down and began to sob.

The doctor didn't offer any words of encouragement. He just stood up and walked out of the room, leaving the scrap of paper with the scribbles he made lying on the floor.

We stayed until about 11:00 P.M. The nurses told us to go and get some sleep, because we'd need our strength later when Chris was awake and needed us. We got hotel rooms and left the hospital with heavy hearts about midnight.

Sleeping was nearly impossible. I cried most of the night. I prayed to God to work a miracle in Chris' life—we needed divine intervention. The doctors were so negative.

Monday, June 12, 2000

I woke early and wanted to get back to the hospital. I didn't want Chris to wake up and not find us there with him. Mike and I arrived at the hospital at 7:00 A.M. I rushed upstairs while Mike went to get me a cup of coffee. I sat by his bed and looked at his body. It was so perfect. He had been through Army boot camp and had been working out. His body was toned, tanned, muscular, and lying perfectly motionless.

I remembered walking through the mall with him over Christmas break. He made such a striking appearance that heads turned as we walked by. Young and old alike turned around to get a second look at him. He knew it and loved it.

"Hey Mom. You see that?" he was referring to the looks he was getting. "It happens to me all the time," he said with a grin.

"Yes, I see that. Think you're something, don't you. Hot Stuff,"

I replied. I wanted to give him a dose of humility, but secretly I was proud that he was so handsome.

I sat by his bed and watched this son I love so much fight for his life. My son's perfect body was broken. His head had a metal halo bolted to it. Fifty pounds of weight were hung to traction his neck and pull the vertebra back into place. He was sedated to keep him calm until surgery. He woke briefly from time to time. We were told that he will not remember anything. He hated the tube down his throat, and fought against it. They had to suction out his lungs to keep his tube clear. He was so scared—I could see it in his eyes. He knew he was fighting to live.

I got phone calls on and off throughout the day, and many visitors. My only focus was Chris. I loved to sit by his side and watch his body breathe. I began to find comfort in the clicking sound. Everyone left me. Mike took Tammy back home to be at graduation practice.

Tuesday, June 13, 2000

God gave me a Bible verse to comfort me while I tried to sleep. "Trust in the Lord with all your heart and lean not unto your own understanding (Proverbs 3:5)." He was telling me not to question why, and not to rely on my very clouded thoughts. I had to trust God to work this situation for His good.

Chris was more agitated and surgery was scheduled for the following day. They needed to stabilize his neck before he did any more damage to his spinal cord. Everyone was getting concerned.

He kept trying to push the tubes out of his mouth with his tongue, because he hated them so much. He moved his head side-to-side violently, trying to get rid of the tubes. We worried about the damage he might have been doing to his neck. They kept giving him more sedation to keep him calm.

One nurse came in while he was thrashing around and

told him that if he pushed the tubes out, he would die. He stared straight at me, with a horrible look on his face, and bit them in half. It was his way of telling me that he didn't want to live like this. The nurse called in help and they re-inserted new tubes. They sent me out, thankfully. It upset me so much to see that look on his face, and to understand his message. I needed time to get myself together again.

Eventually, another resident doctor came to discuss the surgery with us. He described what they needed to do and told us that they had scheduled it for the next day. He said that Dr. White would be performing the surgery because of the seriousness of this injury. I asked when we would meet with Dr. White.

He said, "Oh, Dr. White doesn't talk with anyone. He is Vice President of the hospital and head of Orthopedics. He seldom does surgery, but he never meets with anyone. He doesn't have time."

I told him that absolutely no one would perform surgery on my son unless they had the courtesy of meeting with us first. I needed to see the person I was entrusting my son's life to.

Mom, Dad, and my brother Steve came to be with us. It was really good to see them come through the door. Steve pushed Mom in a wheelchair because she had such trouble walking any distance. I hugged Dad first, and my tears started to flow. He was trying not to let his emotions go, and he looked like he was going to lose the battle.

Just then, Dr. White burst through the doors and into the waiting room. He was followed by an entourage of fledgling doctors. He came over, introduced himself, and shook my hand. He didn't sit down and neither did we. He didn't ask me to introduce any of the other people with me, but he must have assumed they were family because he began to discuss Chris' situation. He told us what he planned regarding the surgical procedure. We asked him a few questions and he gave short, precise answers.

Then he said, "Well, if there aren't any more questions, I'll be on my way."

At that moment, my mother, who quietly sat in her wheelchair during the entire conversation, blurted out, "I've got just one question. Are you that doctor on ER?"

He looked at her and looked back at me. I said, "this is Chris' grandmother." He said nothing. He turned around and walked out, followed by his groupies.

Dad said, "Marcella, what did you do that for?"

I hugged Mom and said, "You sure know how to make an entrance, don't you?" We all laughed just a little through our tears. Then I took them in to see Chris.

When we walked into the room, Chris turned his eyes to his Pepaw and the tears started spilling out. The machine sounded its alarm as he became more agitated and fought through his emotions. Dad's eyes were shinning through his tears, and Mom and Steve were having trouble staying composed as well. Steve was overcome with emotion and had to leave.

I took Mom's hand and kept her beside me. She had decided to walk into Chris' room instead of using her wheelchair. We chatted for just a few minutes and then Mom wasn't able to stand any longer. I walked her back to the waiting room. We left Dad standing there with Chris, rubbing his head and talking that Pepaw talk that the kids have loved all their lives.

We found Steve sitting in the waiting room, sobbing. He was having a really hard time absorbing the situation. We had been through the same thing on Sunday.

Mike and I stayed with Chris until we were totally exhausted, which was around midnight. We were the last ones to leave the hospital. We left hopeful that the surgery tomorrow would bring a miracle.

Wednesday, June 14, 2000

God gave me more hope with yet another Bible verse. "If my people who are called by my name will humble themselves and pray and turn from their wicked ways, then will I hear from heaven and answer their prayers and cleanse them from all unrighteousness." (2 Chronicles 7:14) Did this mean that God would use Chris to bring others to know Him? If all his fraternity brothers mend their ways, would they all be eventually healed? Chris has always had so much influence over so many people. He is truly the happiest person I've ever known. I prayed his accident would not be without benefit.

We sat in the waiting room all day, expectant. Many of our friends, and Chris' friends, came to wait with us. His surgery was finally over at 5:30 P.M. The neck was stabilized and we could only wait until the swelling went down to see how much damage had occurred. I prayed for a complete healing. The doctors told us that his injury is a complete injury with permanent paralysis at C5. He would never walk or use his hands again...so the doctors said. We would not accept this. We held on to the hope that Chris would be healed. It was devastating to us to sit and watch helplessly as a machine breathed for Chris, and tubes of food nourished his body.

Thursday, June 15, 2000

The doctors previously said Chris would come right off the venti-lator because he was so strong. Today they told us they needed to take him back to surgery and do a tracheotomy, which is a more permanent airway to connect him to the ventilator. The tube left in his throat might cause damage to his vocal cords and they now felt he would not be coming off the ventilator so quickly. He was running a fever and having lung problems. I gave them permission and they took him to surgery.

Later that afternoon, they asked to take him back to surgery again and perform a bronchoscopy to suction his lungs deep down where the problem was. They told us he had pneumonia. They changed out his antibiotic to a stronger dose. Chris was heavily sedated because of the two procedures.

We left at the end of the day to go back home for Tammy's graduation the next day. She hadn't been able to participate in any of her senior activities all week, but she didn't complain one bit. Mom, Dad, and Steve went with us.

Friday, June 16, 2000

Tammy's graduation day arrived. She was finished with high school, and glad to be done. We all left the hospital to return home—except her dad, who had stayed behind with Chris.

The hospital called that morning. Chris wasn't getting enough oxygen and the doctors were afraid a blood clot had been thrown to his lungs. They said they needed to do another procedure immediately, and needed my permission. They would run dye thru his lungs to find the clot, and they would also insert something called a basket in the main arteries in his legs. They said it would catch any further clots.

They called back to tell me that he didn't have a blood clot. He had a collapsed left lung. The fluid from the pneumonia filled up his lung, which caused it to collapse. His oxygen levels were very bad. They needed permission to do another procedure, to insert a tube into his left lung through his chest and drain the fluid and re-inflate his lung. I worried that I would lose my son while I was away from him.

It tore me apart inside. Tammy deserved her day, yet Chris was so ill. Patrick called to tell me he was having trouble getting through exams. He needed to see his brother. I told him to come on. We went to Tammy's graduation. Having Memaw, Pepaw, and Steve with us helped make it a special time for Tammy. She had already given up so much that week. We went back to the house after graduation and immediately readied to return to the hospital.

Saturday, June 17, 2000

Chris remained in critical condition. The tension was great. We thought about how special Chris is to us all. It was important for us to remember that we all have a place in his life. Chris continued to run a fever.

I spoke to the doctors about the feeding tubes still in his nose. They irritated him greatly, and I was worried about infection. He certainly didn't need another infection to fight in addition to the pneumonia. They told me that the only alternative was to insert a feeding tube directly in his stomach. If they did this, it would have to remain for at least eight weeks. We agreed it was the best thing to do. So, I gave my permission for yet another procedure.

Sunday, June 18, 2000

One week had passed since the accident, and Chris was still in critical condition. He has always been a fighter. I began to worry about how often he was being sedated. They performed three to four bronchoscopies a day to suction the pneumonia out of his lungs. He hated to see them come in.

It was Father's Day. Mike's son Jonathan brought his girlfriend Amy to visit. They took us to dinner. It felt good to leave the hospital for a while.

Monday, June 19, 200

Patrick arrived. Chris was still critical, and his fever spiked to 103. They still did procedures to get rid of his pneumonia. We worried ceaselessly. He had started saying and seeing crazy things.

He thought he had gone to Florida and Germany. He told me he saw a chinchilla in the room, just sitting over the door smiling at him. He also said he saw chickens coming in the door. I am very concerned about the amount of sedation they have given him. Chris is really hallucinating and I don't think it is funny. One day,

I was standing next to his bed and he got a funny look on his face. His eyes looked slowly all around the room and then he asked me, "how are we going to get down from here?" I told him we'd just walk down. He said, "let's go now."

I was so frightened that I went out after he fell back to sleep and asked to speak to a doctor. I insisted that the sedation be stopped or changed because he was seeing things and I was sure that it wasn't good. The doctors agreed a problem exists. They agreed to lighten up on the sedation.

Mike went back to work, but Patrick and Tammy stayed with me. Chris continued fighting pneumonia.

Tuesday, June 20, 2000

Jennifer Ashby, a high school friend of Chris', came to visit. She offered her apartment to help out. We accepted the offer, agreeing to move into the vacant room on Thursday. Chris was still hallucinating. I wondered how long we could endure this. Everyone prayed for divine intervention.

Wednesday, June 21, 2000

Chris began breathing better, and the antibiotic finally started working. They didn't give Chris any narcotics, so he regained consciousness. They got him out of bed to sit in a reclining chair for brief periods of time. It made his head hurt, and his blood pressure drop dangerously low, but they said it would help his lungs.

He was not happy with his situation at all. I tried to talk with him, telling him not to give up hope. There was no way to know what the future held in store for him. God is always in charge and miracles can happen, regardless of what the doctors say. I told him that we were not going to let this get us down.

Thrusday, June 22, 2000

They moved Chris out of ICU and into a room on the Spinal-Neurology step down unit. We were finally able to stay in the room with him overnight.

Chris' mood was more positive today. He started mouthing words to everyone. He was back to his lovable self again, entertaining everyone who came into his room.

All the nurses love Chris.

Chapter 17

My First Memory

The first conscious thing I remember was opening my eyes and wondering where in the world I was. I looked around an all-white room and instantly a creepy, lonely feeling permeated my thoughts. It was quiet in the room, except for several beeping noises. I was frightened. I began trying to get up. No matter how hard I tried I was unable to move anything. I even remember trying to lift my head, but I couldn't.

I must be in an insane asylum. I thought they had strapped me down to a bed. *I know I'm crazy, but not that crazy.*

Still very confused and disoriented, I looked around at my surroundings again. I noticed that there were foreign objects all over my body. At that point I began to get really scared so I tried to yell out for help, but no noise came out. I tried over and over again to make a sound and was unsuccessful. I started to panic.

About that time, a young woman dressed in scrubs walked into the room. I recognized that she was a nurse and that's when my mind really started wondering. I was confused, and getting angry.

What's going on?

I looked up at her and tried to speak once again. At the same time that I realized I wasn't able to speak, she realized that I was conscious and trying to communicate with her. Seeing my frustration, she put her hand on my arm and leaned over me so that I could see her fully.

Without making a sound I started mouthing to her in a demanding way, "You can take the straps off me now!"

I still hadn't put it all together. I couldn't figure out where I was or what was going on. I was convinced that they had strapped me to the bed. I wasn't thinking about the possibility that I was paralyzed. For that matter, I didn't even consider that I might have an injury.

Tears formed in the young nurse's eyes. She took a deep breath, pulled herself together, and managed to say, "There are no straps on you, honey. You have been in a very severe car accident and are not able to move."

I was so shocked I wasn't able to comprehend what was happening. The nurse started crying and ran out of the room. Later I learned that it was her first week as a nurse. I can't imagine what it must have been like for her to be a nurse straight out of college. It must have been hard treating a man so close to her age and to see one of her first patients broken, and so vulnerable.

Minutes later a doctor came into the room with a clipboard full of medical charts. We soon began to call him "the pit bull" because of his manners. He stood beside my bed and spoke with an intimidating almost foreign-sounding voice.

"Mr. Skinner you have suffered a spinal cord injury at the level of C5–C6 and you're paralyzed. The beeping sound that you hear is a ventilator that is enabling you to breathe. Due to the swelling of your neck we had to perform a tracheotomy. You may never be able to breathe on your own again. You may not be able to move your arms again and you will never walk again."

He continued to talk, explaining my situation in more depth. I had started crying hysterically after hearing the words, "never walk again." I kept thinking over and over in my mind that this wasn't happening to me; this doctor reeling off the reality of my situation was just a figment of my imagination, and this whole situation was just one big nightmare from which I would soon wake.

Unfortunately I was awake, and this was the situation that I had to deal with. I started to panic, and felt like my entire body was squeezing tighter and tighter on me. Fortunately, my mother, who I lovingly refer to as my pit bull, was in the room with me. She had just about all the negativity that she could take. She stood to her feet like a soldier given an order straight from the president. She asked the doctor to leave the room.

She marched right over to me, leaned over and told me that the doctor was wrong. With her jaw gritted and her fist clenched tightly she looked me in the eyes.

"Chris, that doctor is wrong," she said, "No one on the face of this planet can tell you what you can or cannot do! They don't know. They can tell you what your situation is right now. But only God has complete authority and power over all of life. Through Him, I believe all things are possible!"

Then she told me about my accident and my surgery. She told me what day it was. She talked about my injuries and told me the truth. She said, "no one really knows how things will turn out. These doctors only know how to deal with what they see right now. But you and I are going to have faith and stay positive. We are going to continue believing and praying that your situation will change and that you will be healed."

"Do you understand that, Chris?" she asked.

I just stared at her and nodded my head "yes." At that point, I felt much more at ease. I didn't necessarily buy into the whole God-scenario, but at the time, lying on my back, I only wanted to hear about the positive possibilities.

I had so much to deal with all at once. I was lying in a bed in a hospital unable to move. I was hooked up to machines and they were breathing for me and eating for me and basically keeping me alive. I couldn't even move my arms to scratch my nose. It was like I was trapped in my body. There wasn't anything I could do except go with the flow.

I spent the day trying to remember what I could of the time before my accident. I had absolutely no recollection of anything after the paramedics arrived on the scene. I suppose I should be thankful for that.

Since I was fully conscious now, everyone wanted to talk with me. I saw more doctors and nurses that day. They came in teams into my room and asked me tons of questions and turned around and left. I just wanted to be left alone. Since I was still in ICU, visitors were limited. I guess you could say I was very unsociable that day, trying to take it all in. My girlfriend told my mother that I was the devil himself. I was really mean to her, telling her to go away. I wanted everyone to go away and let me die. I just didn't know how I could possibly live under these circumstances.

The next day I was sent to the Spinal-Neurology step down unit. I could now have visitors in my room all the time. In fact, someone could sleep in my room at night. My mom slept the first of many nights on a cot in my room. I woke her up every two hours, crying and telling her I just couldn't do this. I couldn't handle this. She patiently reassured me that there was nothing we were ever asked to handle that we didn't also receive the strength to do so. She said that God was holding us both in the palm of His hands and wouldn't let us go through this situation alone. We just had to trust Him.

I didn't want to hear any of that. I just wanted to wake up from this nightmare and walk out of it. I wanted to escape from the consequences of my actions, like always. Only this time, there was no way out.

Chapter 18

Get Ready

The main goal of the step down unit was to prepare me for Acute Rehab. There were some additional evaluations to be done, now that I was no longer in critical condition. I had appointments with Occupational Therapists, Physical Therapists, and therapists to evaluate my other bodily functions, to see just what I could still do.

One of the first tests they gave me when I got to the step down unit was a swallow test to determine if the muscles in my throat would still function enough to allow me to resume eating and drinking normally. For twenty-one days, I wasn't able to have anything to eat or drink. After I awoke, I begged them to allow me to sip some water. They would not allow me to swallow anything until I had a swallow test.

As I mentioned before, all my nourishment was going through a feeding tube inserted directly into my stomach, which provided "food." At least that's what they called it. A bag of liquid sustenance hung above my bed and hooked into the tube that drained into my body. Not exactly like eating pizza, or burgers and fries! They actually had different flavors and colors of the stuff. Of course I wasn't able to taste what was going in, so it seemed silly.

The tube and the bag of "food" were there to provide my body with the amount of nutrients that it needed to survive. I often tried to make light out of the situation. When the nurses came in to fill it up, I'd mouth to them, "I'd like steak and a baked potato, please."

At first they didn't know how to react. After they got to know me, they would giggle and grant my wish in a joking manner.

It was absolute torture watching people eat meals and have drinks. I was so hungry and thirsty that I would have dreams about going out to eat with friends. After communicating this with my mother, she made sure that no one ate or drank in my presence. One day my mom basically kicked my brother out of the room to eat his breakfast elsewhere, so that it wouldn't bother me. After that, no one would eat in the room in front of me, because they knew I wanted to eat so badly.

The reason I wasn't able to eat any solid food, or drink any fluids, was that the doctors had to make sure that what I swallowed did not go into my lungs. In order to find out whether or not I was capable of correctly swallowing food and drinking fluids, I had to pass a certain test in which I ate food and drank fluids that were saturated with barium. To give you an idea of what barium tastes like, imagine taking a bite out of freshly mixed cement—yum!

When they tested me, they were able to trace the barium-laced food and drink as it traveled through my body by looking at an x-ray machine while I swallowed. My dad went with me and we were both able to watch the food and drink go down into my stomach.

The whole week before this test, I had been telling everyone that I couldn't wait to eat. All I wanted was a cheeseburger. I was anticipating the moment, knowing that the food would taste so good. When I finally passed the swallow test and was given the green light, I came back to my room anxious to eat my cheeseburger.

My Uncle Douglas went down to the cafeteria and got me a cheeseburger. He made sure it had ketchup, my favorite topping. He came back and fed me the first bite. The room was full of family members, and they were all waiting to see the look of pleasure on my face.

UGH! I thought. *That tastes awful.* My cheeseburger tasted nothing like a cheeseburger.

Because of the tracheotomy, I had gotten thrush, a kind of fungus, on my tongue and the back of my throat. Thrush can develop in people who have weakened immune systems, like babies or people who take large doses of antibiotics. Each day, they painted medicine in my mouth and down my throat to kill this fungus. The fungus wasn't all it killed. My taste buds had been affected as well. I just hadn't realized it because I hadn't had real food or drink for so long. The cementy barium concoctions didn't count.

When I took that first bite of the cheeseburger, it tasted like cardboard. Two bites were all I managed to eat. I was so let down, and everyone else was disappointed for me.

Eventually, the evaluations were finished and I was ready for rehab, with the exception of my fever. I had to be free from a fever for twenty-four hours before I could be allowed to go. I had been on antibiotics for almost as long as I had been in the hospital. I battled pneumonia constantly.

During my surgery, they'd removed all the IV lines and converted them to one main line that was inserted in my chest. This was a somewhat permanent tube, inserted into a main vein in my chest. They put these tubes in for chemo and dialysis patients, and for any patient who needs frequent injections of fluids, meds, etc. All my meds went through this line. It was the last thing to be taken out. Fortunately, after it was removed, the fever instantly went away. I was ready to go to Acute Rehab.

Chapter 19

Acute Rehab

When something of this magnitude happens, you might think you are going through it all by yourself. You feel all alone. That couldn't be further from the truth. Your family, friends and even people that you don't know are affected by your situation. They are going through it with you. In some cases, they take on most of the initial difficulties. This was the case with my situation. I had no idea what my parents were going through at that time. My mom said that she just wanted me to focus my energies on getting my body better. She would take care of worrying about the details. There were more details to worry about than you might imagine.

While I was in the step down unit, my parents were told that they would need to make preparations with a rehab center for me. My mother worked with the health insurance company to see what was in our network. She and my step-dad, Mike, visited the center close to the hospital in Charlottesville, VA and one in Richmond, VA. They went online to find which rehab center had the best reputation.

My mother talked with people at Shepherd's in Atlanta, GA, and was convinced that this was the right choice for me. The question was whether the insurance would cover it. It was also out-of-state and we needed to know if Department of Rehabilitative Services (DRS) would cover a non-Virginia facility. She talked with our case manager at the insurance company about this situation, and DRS. She called Shepherd and worked out all the details.

It was a go. I was going to one of the best facilities with a great reputation, and still be in-network. There I could do my acute rehab, then transition right into the more long-term rehab. They even had apartment units where my mother and I could live together while I underwent therapy.

I had no idea about all the details that had to be solved. All I knew, basically, was that whatever I wanted happened. When my mother told me about what she had accomplished for me, I shot it down. I said in no uncertain terms that I was not going to Georgia, especially not for three to six months. That was too long to be that far away from my friends. I needed to see them, and I knew for a fact that none of them would go to Georgia to see me. I certainly didn't want to be forgotten. I was also afraid of losing my girlfriend. So I said no. I wanted to go to rehab in Charlottesville.

My mother said "okay," and made it happen. Two days later, I was transported by ambulance to Health South Rehab Center in Charlottesville, VA. We didn't realize what a difference a change of facilities would make to our feelings. Leaving the familiar UVA Medical Center, which had been our security throughout this experience was difficult. We entered a new and unknown setting, and it really unnerved both my mother and me. We had been told that this would be tough. We just didn't realize how tough.

When my mother, toured the facility and made the arrangements for me, they had shown her a private room, close to the nurses' station. They told her that I would be in that room, since I was still on the ventilator. When I got there, they took me to another room that I would share with another young man about my age. They said they thought I would enjoy having the company. They also said that I would not be able to have anyone stay with me at night.

I remember the doctors and nurses talking about me

while still in my presence, as if I were not a person. They used unfamiliar terms like "quad." I had a panic attack. I started crying and told my mother that I just couldn't get through this if she left me. I told her that I was afraid. I let out a lot of the feelings I had been covering up.

It was such an overwhelming experience: a new environment, a new routine, and a new way of living. I had to depend on so many people for my survival that my confidence was shattered. I didn't know how I was going to survive or how I was going to adjust to everything. It seemed like every time I had to make a change and adapt to a new routine, I broke down.

People are like that. When change comes knocking at our doors and we don't know how to respond, we start to panic. It is completely understandable to feel like this, but we need to remember that change is sometimes for the better.

My mother stood there by my bed me and comforted me. She promised me that she would not leave me, and that she would work things out. And she did. Shortly thereafter, we moved into the room that was promised me, and they brought a chair that flipped out into a bed so that I could have someone stay with me.

I was comforted, but not entirely. I still had to face all my other challenges. The first doctor to walk through my door asked me, "How do you spell rehab?"

To communicate, I had to mouth words and letters. I could blink to answer yes or no questions. It was frustrating to be unable to talk. My audience had to read my lips to understand what I was trying to say.

So I mouthed the answer. "R-E-H-A-B."

The doctor said, "Nope. W-O-R-K! Get ready."

I'm the kind of guy who really likes a challenge. The doctor's challenge got my attention. I decided that he was on. I'd take everything they threw my way, and I'd walk out of this place.

The next day, there was a meeting with my parents, my doctors, my therapists, the nursing director, and me. It was an intake meeting. They went over their programs, and asked me if I had any questions. They said they would teach me how to do everyday things in a new way, using my limited resources. They said their plan could change as my physical condition changed.

I had two major goals that would have to be accomplished simultaneously. The first goal was to be able to sit in a wheelchair, which would enable me to have mobility to accomplish everything else. The second goal, equally important, was to be weaned off the ventilator, if possible. There were many other goals to consider, but they were all dependent on these two major accomplishments.

Chapter 20

I Want To Talk About Me

As you can imagine, this whole experience was the most painful and horrifying of my life, especially because of the ventilator. Because of the machine, it was extremely hard for me to communicate. All of my life I have been outspoken, but here I was, unable to make even the smallest sound. We developed a system in which everyone spoke to me in the form of yes or no questions. That way I could answer by blinking once for yes and twice for no. It was frustrating, and I got so tired of blinking my eyes.

Sometimes, it was impossible to communicate with yes and no questions, so I tried to mouth the words to answer. This, too, was difficult and frustrating. We even had to go as far as breaking some words down letter by letter. At times, it might take half an hour to communicate one word to someone.

It was fortunate that one of the first things we accomplished in rehab was to give me a better way to communicate. It would take a while for me to wean off the breathing machine and they wanted me to be able to talk. They replaced the valve cover on my tracheotomy with a speaking valve. It was a small, circular plastic piece with a screen-like material over its end. It worked almost like a Kazoo, except somehow you could make clear words come out. I would take a deep breath in and blow out through it and it acted like an artificial vocal cord. It was amazing, but very difficult to master.

At first, I didn't have enough breath to make it work properly. All I could do was make funny quacking noises that sounded like Donald Duck. I had a hard time learning to breathe in and talk while my breath was coming out. It also dried my throat out so much that I really didn't like to use it. I wouldn't talk very much, and when I did, I spoke with really short sentences.

The first time I successfully made it work correctly, my mom wasn't with me. She had gone to the Long John Silver's restaurant to bring me back some dinner. The traffic had been terrible, and it took her longer than normal to return. She rushed back into the room, exhausted and flustered. My room was full of relatives, and I had planned to surprise Mom by speaking to her.

"What took you so long?" I asked.

She walked across the room, unpacked my meal from the bag, and put it on the table by my bed. Without thinking, she started to answer my question.

"The traffic was…"

Then it dawned on her that I had spoken.

"OH, MY GOSH!! You spoke! Chris, you spoke!" she exclaimed. She was so excited. We all laughed together.

For the rest of the evening, no one could shut me up, even if they had wanted to. I was finally able to communicate my thoughts and feelings freely. I talked on and on about anything that came into my mind. I entertained everyone with my new voice, which I sometimes used for a Donald Duck impression, just for a laugh.

Chapter 21

Work—They Weren't Kidding

I was ready for my next big rehab challenge. I had enormous problems with my blood pressure. It was extremely low, averaging 70/40 (a normal blood pressure reading is around 120/80). Because my blood pressure was so low, I felt sick. I experienced dizziness and nausea in any position I took, other than lying down.

When my physical therapist tried to sit me up, my blood pressure would drop even lower and I would pass out. My body couldn't handle it. My vision would slowly fade to black and I would lose my hearing. As you can imagine, I didn't want to get up because I felt so horrible every time I tried. When the therapist would come to get me, I would cry. I didn't want to go through the whole process of passing out.

Finally, I realized that the longer I stayed on my back, the longer it would take to get used to sitting up straight. With that in mind, every morning I decided to grit my teeth and continue trying. At first it was a miserable, repetitive process. They sat me up and I passed out. Over and over again we went through this routine: sit up, pass out, sit up, pass out.

The therapist tried different methods to help me. She put support hose on my legs, and wrapped them tightly in ace bandages to keep the blood from staying in my legs. Ultimately, it all came down to sheer willpower and persistence. After about a week and a half, I sat up straight in my wheelchair. Although the process was miserable, and sitting in the wheelchair for the first time made me feel sick, I smiled with a sense of accomplishment. I had set a goal, and even though it was a tough

Chris (8 mos)

Family Portrait 1983
Patrick (7), Chris (3), Tammy (8 mos)

Batter up (2 yrs)

T-Ball (5 yrs)

Chris reading (3 yrs)

Boogie Boarding

Waterskiing (13 yrs)

Rec Soccer (10 yrs)

Apple Picking—Chris (14), Jonathan (13),
Mom & Tammy (12)

Christmas 1995—Tammy (13),
Mike, Mom, Chris (16), Patrick (19
w/long hair), Johnathan (14)

Tammy & Chris (blondes)

Christmas 1996

Chris & Dad—Hiking
Grandfather Mountain

Senior Prom 1997
Jennifer & Chris

Hula Contest Winner
(DECA Seminar 1997, FL)

Just Chillin'

High School Graduate
1997

126 Varsity Wrestling 9th grade

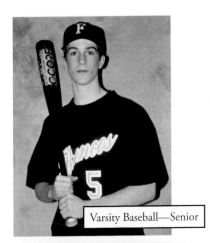

Varsity Baseball—Senior

Varsity Basketball—Senior

Varsity Golf—Senior

Canoeing

Snorkeling—Chris & Kelly

Fishing—Florida Keys

127

Josh, Chris & Freshmen Suitemates—
Anthony, Jason, Mike, Ryan

Chris with
friend Adam

Army Boot Camp—May 1999

Chris Returning home from boot camp—
August 1999

June 10, 2000—
two hours before
accident

Christmas 1999—
Patrick & Chris

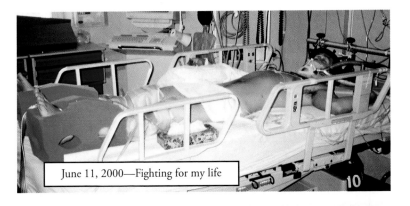

June 11, 2000—Fighting for my life

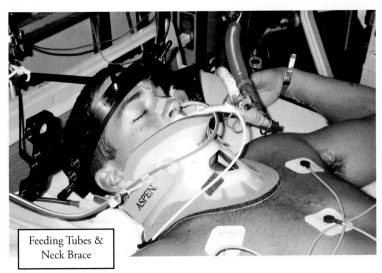

Feeding Tubes & Neck Brace

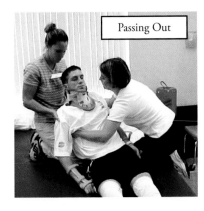

Passing Out

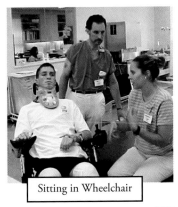

Sitting in Wheelchair

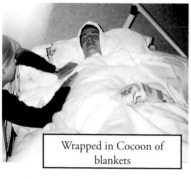

Wrapped in Cocoon of blankets

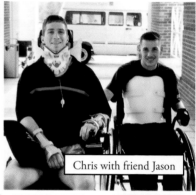

Chris with friend Jason

Driver training at McGuire Veterans Hospital

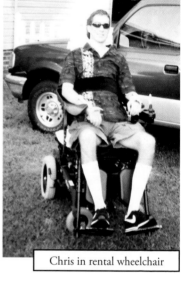

Chris in rental wheelchair

Ceramics at WWRC

Therapy at home—Painting with Tammy

Chris' Masterpiece

Moving in Dorm Room with Mike's Help

Chris & Robin (Obi-Wan) Clark enjoying the view

June 2001—One Year After Accident

Brian, Chris & Tammy—Sept. 29, 2001

Micah, Chris, Noah Christopher (namesake) & Suzanne

RU Graduation Day with Family

Getting the long awaited diploma from
Dr. Covington—December 2002

RU Grad

Chris writing this book with
voice activated software

Chris speaks to high school students

Chris speaks to high school students

Chris speaks to RU Alumni

Chris encourages kids at College Bound Conference (VA Tech)

Chris addresses educators at AHEAD Conference

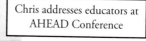

Chris & his Dad (Wayne) at Tammy's wedding

Memaw, Chris, Suzie & Pepaw

Was that a winner?

Learning to Sail, 2001

Tammy, Mom, Patrick, Chris holding nephew Blake, 2003

Playing chess with Suzie

Day at VA Beach with friend, Robin, June 2002

Ask Suzie to marry me
(She said Yes!)
June 10, 2003

Chris stands to kiss his bride (with help of groomsmen)

Chris marries Suzie

Chris & Suzie at VA Beach

Chris & Suzie swim in pool at VA Beach
resort...and life goes on...

road, I managed to accomplish it. I had taken a positive step in the right direction.

I believe life is all about goals. Each of us should set our goals as high as we can dream, and go after them with all of our heart, mind, and soul. Remember, the only person who can stop us from accomplishing our goals is ourselves. However, we must remember to be patient when we set our goals. Sometimes the only way to achieve is to take things one day at a time, and move forward with one foot in front of the other.

A lot of times, we want instant gratification. The feeling is completely normal. But for the most part, life doesn't work that way. Remember, for example, that people don't become doctors overnight. They attend school for years, and train carefully and tirelessly. No matter how much we want to reach our goal quickly, we have to be patient. We have to grit our teeth, keep pressing forward, have faith, and believe in our ability to accomplish.

Even though I accomplished my goal of sitting up straight that day, I still battle the same dizziness and nausea that I felt in the beginning. Thanks to medication, these feelings aren't nearly as bad as they were initially, but they still exist. It is especially hard for me when I wake up in the morning, and sit up for the first time each day. Sometimes it takes a while for my body to adjust to the upright sitting position. But I refuse to let a little dizziness stop me from living my life, and reaching my goals. That is how it should be for you. Don't let the little details distract you from achieving.

Once I was able to sit up in the wheelchair, my rehab program evolved. My typical day started at 7:00 A.M. when a nurse came into my room, turned on the lights, and opened the blinds. I am definitely not a morning person, so this angered me beyond belief. Some mornings it felt like a flashback to boot camp when the drill sergeants came in banging trashcans at 4:00 A.M.

A clinical aid provided by the facility fed me breakfast, got me dressed, and helped me out of bed and into my wheelchair. This process took one to two hours, depending on various circumstances that arose. Once in my wheelchair, I rolled into the physical therapy gym. There, the therapist took me out of the wheelchair and laid me on a mat.

This process used to really bother me. By the time I wheeled into PT, my blood pressure would have finally acclimated to sitting up straight. And the first thing they did was lie me back down. I'd have to go through the same process of getting used to sitting up at the end of the session. It seemed like all I did was get up and lie down, over and over again, all day long.

Once I was on the mat, the therapist stretched my legs and arms. We followed that with an exercise regimen that concentrated on movement techniques and strengthening exercises. My movement was slow to return but I worked at it faithfully. I held on to the hope that I could recover more as my therapy progressed. I had already seen a lot of progress already.

When I first awoke from the accident, I was unable to move either of my arms. Several weeks later, while I lay in the bed, my left arm started twitching. Everyone got very excited and encouraged me to keep twitching it, which I did. I would lie in the bed and stare at my left arm, trying to move it, hour after hour. Finally, I reached the point where I could flip my palm up. My family and friends would turn my palm down and I would flip it over on my own. We exercised it like this for days. As I continued flipping my hand back and forth, I began to get more and more function in my left arm. Eventually I was able to move the entire arm.

After establishing some sort of motor control in my left arm, I concentrated on my right arm. I began reaching over with my left arm and going through the movements I had been using. I forced my right hand to flip back and forth, just like

I had done with my left. After several days of this, I miraculously felt a twitch in my right arm. I continued exercising it until I was able to move it almost as well as my left arm. This process took months to accomplish and extended beyond my time at Health South. Unfortunately, since I fractured my right scapula and severely damaged the surrounding ligaments in the accident, I experienced immense pain every time I moved my right arm. Although it was painful, and not nearly as strong as my left arm, I was still satisfied that I had recovered some function.

When it was time to finish my stretches and exercises, the PT put me back in the wheelchair and I went to occupational therapy. My rehab day continued right on schedule. The purpose of occupational therapy was to teach me how to live as a quadriplegic person, using adaptive equipment in order to gain independence. I felt like I was being forced to learn how to live, and function as a human being, all over again.

The therapist put braces on me and tried to teach me to brush my teeth and shave myself. I didn't want to do it. I just wanted to cry. I didn't like the idea of being a handicapped person who had to do everything with braces, or with the help of another person. I didn't like being seen wearing adaptive equipment. It made me feel so dependent and ugly. I couldn't grasp the two virtues I needed most, which were determination and patience. I wasn't determined, yet.

"This isn't happening to me," I kept saying to myself. "I don't have to learn this crap because I'm going to get better. I'm going to walk out of this stupid rehab place one day. I'm going to brush my teeth again the way I used to. I don't need to learn this way. I don't need to waste my time playing with all of this annoying adaptive equipment!"

I simply couldn't and wouldn't accept what had happened to me. I was still fighting the mental battle that came with my injury. I was mad at the world. I was mad at God. I was mad at myself. I hadn't yet hit the place where I was determined to deal with my situation, and re-learn how to do things. I really didn't put my heart into what I was doing because I was expecting things to change and miraculously get better.

Even though I thought my situation wouldn't last, I hated the fact that I was being negative and feeling depressed. As re-hab continued, this bothered me more and more. I had always adjusted to hard and negative situations fairly well before. I was, and am, a person who wants to be the best at whatever task is set forth. I began to motivate myself and force myself to think positively. I told myself over and over, "I'm going to beat this."

Although I was still in denial, I didn't want the current situation to get the best of me. I dug deep and found the determination I needed. Have you heard the phrase, "When life gives you lemons, make lemonade?" Well, I was going to try and make some lemonade.

There will always be bad situations. We will always face adversity in our lives. It is just a fact. The most important thing we can do in bad situations is figure out how to make something good happen as a result. It boils down to attitude! If we can hold on to a positive attitude and let go of our negative attitude, we can take steps forward and change things for the better.

I had so many situations to deal with all at once, each trying every last nerve in my body. Even so, I forced myself to wake up with a good attitude, grit my teeth, and give myself a pep talk.

"All right Chris. You're going to get up and you're going to pass out. Then you're going to get up again. You're going to keep doing this until you can sit up. You're going to pick up that toothbrush and you're going to keep trying until you can brush your teeth. You're going to take that fork and keep trying until you can pick up that food and get it to your mouth. You're going to learn to write. You're going to walk again."

I tried as hard as I could. After many failures, some ending with food in my lap or toothpaste all over my face, I started to get the hang of things.

Chapter 22

To Eat Again

They continued feeding me through the stomach tube, at the same time encouraging me to eat what came on my meal tray. The food tasted horrible to me so I didn't eat much. I lost over fifty pounds. They couldn't take me off the feeding tube until I was eating enough to sustain myself. Every evening, someone would come into my room carrying a clipboard and ask me to recall exactly what I had eaten and drank that day. Then they would always tell me that I wasn't eating enough to get off the feeding tube and would have to keep it in until I was eating enough.

I had to make a decision about whether or not I wanted to be independent of the liquid being poured directly into my stomach. I decided to start eating. Regardless of the taste, I would eat.

Along with the decision to eat, I decided to take my meals in dining area with the other patients. This was a big step for me. I still wasn't very good at getting the food to my mouth on a consistent basis. I didn't want to drop food all over myself with everyone around watching me. Eating in the dining area turned out to be better than I expected.

Everyone was in pretty much the same situation. They all needed assistance from others, or from adaptive devices, to feed themselves. I remember one day they sat me at the table in front of an elderly Italian man who had injured his back and had a metal halo bolted into his skull. His injury would eventually heal, the contraption would be removed, and he'd be able to walk again. He was a kind and compassionate man, one who loved to eat.

The meal that day consisted of spaghetti, green beans, a salad, and garlic bread. He was really enjoying his lunch. None of the food had much taste to me. I never looked forward to my meals. When the man noticed me picking at my meal, he spoke up.

"You must-a eat boy," he said in a very thick accent. "You get strong and go home."

I told him I really didn't like the taste of the food, but I was doing the best that I could. He noticed that I had hardly touched the green beans.

"Put some vin-a-ger on those beans. Make them taste good. You eat then. Yes?"

I didn't quite understand what he was telling me to put on the green beans. Apparently, I looked puzzled. I looked at my mother to see if she understood. The man's wife, who was sitting beside him repeated the word "vin-a-ger" and gestured towards the beans.

I repeated the word they said, "vin-a-ger," several times and they shook their heads in unison vigorously.

"Yes. Yes." they said.

Finally, Mom and I got it, almost at the same time.

"Vinegar!" we said in unison. The man and his wife continued nodding their heads, this time smiling.

Mom said, "Oh. We have some in the room left over from your Long John Silver meal the other night."

She ran back to my room and brought back several packets. We put some on my beans and shared with the man across from me. He eagerly stuck his fork into the beans and munched away on them.

"That's-a good," he exclaimed.

I decided to try mine, and found he was right. I was able

to taste the beans. After that day, I kept packets of vinegar, Texas Pete hot sauce, and ketchup to put on all my meals. I had found something I could actually taste.

Finally, they told me that I was eating enough on my own to be able take the tube out. However, they couldn't take the tube out yet. What a let down. I had achieved my goal, but didn't win the prize.

When they put a feeding tube into the stomach, it goes through the stomach lining. The reason they couldn't take it out was that my lining had to completely heal around it before they could pull the tube out. If we didn't wait, I would hemorrhage. Time is a major factor in the healing process. It would take at least eight weeks before it could safely be removed.

The tube was there to stay for a while longer. They capped it off and taped it to my skin. This also caused problems. I was allergic to the tape and so my skin stayed irritated. One day, when the doctor was in visiting, I asked him how he was going to get it out.

He told me, "I'm just going to pull it out."

I then asked, "How are you going to pull it out?"

He teased me, saying, "I'm going to stick my foot on your stomach and pull it right out."

"Man, you're crazy," I said.

One day, he came in and asked, "Are you ready?"

"Yup," I said.

I always liked watching them work on me. Sometimes, I would yell "Ouch," just to see their reaction. I actually couldn't feel anything they did below my shoulders, but they always forgot. I was able to scare lots of nurses, doctors, and even my mother. It was something I did to amuse myself, and it got a few laughs from others as well.

He took a syringe and deflated the balloon that held the tube in place inside in my stomach. He wrapped the tube around his hand.

He said, "One, two three," and pulled.

The tube went "POP" and came right out of my stomach. This time it was my turn to be on the receiving end. I was so scared that I forgot to yell "Ouch."

I asked him, "How will you know if my stomach is healing properly and I'm not bleeding to death?"

He answered, "Oh, we will know in a few days, after you use the bathroom a couple of times. If there is blood in your stools, we'll know then."

I looked at him in disbelief and said, "There has to be a better way than that."

Miraculously, the hole eventually did close by itself, and I didn't have any problems at all with bleeding. I continued to eat, with the knowledge that I must to stay alive. I couldn't feel hunger, and even my vinegar and hot sauce couldn't help the taste of all my meals.

Chapter 23

Breathe

Being dependent on a ventilator to breathe scared me to death. The main goal of my acute rehab was to wean me off. I wanted to breathe on my own, and get off that machine.

What I hated the most was suctioning. This process had to be done in order to keep my lungs clear of mucus, and to prevent pneumonia and other dangerous infections. Every three to four hours, more frequently if necessary, a respiratory therapist came into my room and performed the procedure. It was so painful that when I heard the respiratory therapist walking down the hall, I would cry like a newborn baby.

The respiratory therapist used a long red tube that was part of a vacuum-like machine attached to the wall beside my bed. They took the gauze off my neck, removed the ventilator, and inserted the suctioning tube down the open hole in my throat (the tracheotomy), underneath my Adam's apple . They continued to push the tube in and out, down my throat, until it reached the bottom of my lungs and all of the mucus was suctioned out. It felt like a hot poker gashing the back of my throat and deep down into my chest. Sometimes the process took much longer than other times.

No matter how many times they suctioned, and no matter how long it took to finish the process, I cried and gagged the whole time, every time. It was one of the most painful things I have ever had to undergo in my life. I didn't know how much more of this pain I could bear, so I wanted to wean off the ventilator as soon as possible. After talking to the doctors, we set up a schedule to start my venture of breathing on my own again.

To begin the weaning process, they turned the ventilator off for short periods of time, allowing me to breathe using my own muscles. When I became fatigued, they reattached the ventilator to give me a rest. I remember that first time off of the ventilator like it was yesterday. I can't describe how scary it was to feel completely dependent on a machine for survival. When they turned it off, it felt like someone had put their hands around my neck and squeezed my throat closed. On that first go around, I only made it for two minutes before I begged them to put me back on the machine.

I remember mouthing, "I can't breathe! I can't breathe!" as my face turned bright purple.

They immediately reattached my foe, the evil ventilator. After I regained my composure, my determination kicked in. I wanted to give it another shot. I made a decision that no matter how hard it was or how long it took, I was going to beat that machine and gain my independence.

For the second trial, I tried to relax myself an hour or so beforehand. This time, I managed to breathe successfully on my own for a full thirty minutes. I was exhausted after the thirty minutes of breathing on my own, but instead of focusing on my fatigue I began thinking and preparing for the next trial.

The therapist and I worked together to continue the weaning process throughout the day, every day, for the next several weeks. Every time they detached the ventilator I managed to breathe alone for longer periods of time. They told me I had to work my way up to twenty-four hours, and then I would be off. It was hard work. I was amazed at the amount of energy it took to train my body to breathe again.

While I weaned myself from the ventilator, I needed the help of family and friends. Someone always stayed in the room to make sure that I was breathing. Sometimes I dozed off and my body forgot to breathe. When I stopped breathing, I'd turn blue and start choking and gasping for air. Often I was lucky, and a relative or friend got my attention before I reached the point that I stopped breathing. As you can imagine, the idea of suffocating was pretty scary for me, and for the person staying with me. We all tried to stay calm and get through it.

I was terribly frightened about being off the ventilator, unable to catch my breath and completely helpless, but every time I thought about being suctioned, I felt more compelled to go forward. I would stay calm, focusing on my next step, and my next goal. I remember saying to myself each and every time I started to become afraid or anxious, "Focus Skinner, you can do this!"

I couldn't take deep breaths, because the damage to my spinal cord left me with nerve stimulation in only the top fifty percent of my lungs, making it impossible for me to inflate the lower half of my lungs. No one was sure that I was going to be able to come completely off the machine, but me. I had almost no diaphragm muscles to use. My body had to get a certain amount of oxygen to function properly or I would have to remain on the machine. I was determined to get off that machine.

I had to work on taking deeper breaths to provide enough oxygen to my body. I had to do breathing exercises several times a day. I would blow into a Spirometer, a machine that measured the amount of airflow in my lungs. As I blew, I watched a ball go up and down a cylindrical-shaped tube. The goal was to blow the ball to the top line, and make it stay there as long as possible. Along with the Spirometer exercises, the therapist placed five-pound weights on my diaphragm while I held deep breaths. We completed several repetitions of this exercise during therapy. We gradually increased the weights to ten pounds. I worked hard and exercised daily, and it soon started to pay off. As each day passed, my stamina increased and so did my confidence. I felt like now I was fighting on a more level battlefield and gaining momentum. I wasn't going to give up until I won the battle completely.

It was a long emotional, physical, and mental battle to be completely independent from the machine for a full twenty-four hours. I was so used to depending on a machine for every breath that each time they removed it, I became frightened and would sometimes panic. It took such an enormous amount of energy that I got to the point where all I could do was focus on breathing. It was incredibly difficult to take deep breaths. It felt like someone was sitting on top of me.

To overcome this, I started to mentally visualize a very large person sitting on my chest. Each time I made a positive step in my breathing, the person lost weight and became lighter. This helped me focus my energy and control my fears as I took deeper and deeper breaths. As I progressed, I began to despise the thought of going back on the ventilator at the end of the day. It seemed to me that every time I used the ventilator I became reliant on it all over again, making it that much harder to take it off for the next trial.

Finally, I reached the point where I was able to breathe on my own for twenty hours. It was 2:00 A.M. I needed to be catheterized and to be turned from side to side to prevent pressure sores every two hours. The respiratory therapist usually came to check on my breathing at the same time as the nurse. The respiratory therapist began prepping the ventilator, getting ready to reattach it.

She said, "You've done great! Oxygen levels are in normal range. You've gone twenty hours. Now, it is time to put you back on the ventilator for a rest."

At that point I had had enough. I decided that I was going to go for it!

All or nothing, I thought. *I know I can do this! I just have to concentrate hard enough and stay calm.*

When the therapist turned to me I shook my head no, gritted my teeth, and began crying. I looked the therapist dead in the eyes.

"I refuse to get back on that ventilator!" I shouted. "I am going to make it!"

I pleaded my case, explaining my feelings about the ventilator. I knew that at this point in the trial, it only made me weaker and more reliant to put that evil machine back on.

She said, "Nope. You're going back on."

"Each time you put me back on that machine now, it makes it twice as hard for me to come back off. My body gets used to being without it and I don't like the way it makes me feel when it starts back up. It's like my whole body is fighting with the machine now," I tried to explain to her.

"You have to go back on!" she said emphatically.

"There is no way I am going back on it! You all tell me to direct my care, so I am. I refuse to go back on that machine." I said.

She said, "You are going to make me lose my job if you don't go back on the machine. I have written orders and I can't allow you to stay off that machine."

After a couple minutes of arguing, going through hospital rules, regulations, and logistics, she turned and went out of the room.

In a few minutes, she returned and said, "Okay. I won't put you back on it, but I am writing in your chart that 'patient refused therapy.'"

She made me acknowledge a patient refusal letter, which was placed in my chart, relinquishing them from liability.

I said, "Fine…and thanks."

I had refused it. I stayed off the ventilator that night and watched every minute tick off the clock until twenty-four hours had passed and I had accomplished my goal. From that point on, the ventilator never touched my throat again, and I was able to breathe freely on my own. My therapist kept checking on me all through the night to make sure I was all right. I was very worn down and tired. She had to bring in oxygen and give me a little extra from time to time during the night, and all through the next day.

I wasn't able to get out of bed that day to do my normal activities, because it was taking everything I had just to breathe. But I did it! It had taken over eight weeks, but I had weaned myself from the ventilator. My therapist was thrilled for me as well. But I wasn't out of the woods yet.

Now that I had achieved the goal of being independent from the ventilator, it was up to me to keep my lungs strong. They were all worried about fluid building up because I wasn't inflating the bottom sections of my lungs. Before they would remove my tracheotomy, which would mean they could no longer suction my lungs, they had to make sure I could clear my lungs of phlegm on my own. They started teaching me a procedure called "quad coughing." My mother had to learn the procedure, too. A person must put his or her hands on my diaphragm and perform thrusts in an upward angle to force air out and help me cough, blow my nose, etc. It is basically the same thing as performing the Heimlich maneuver on a small child.

We had to work to learn this procedure to protect my lungs. All during this process, they kept the tracheotomy in my neck, covered with a plug, in case they had to put me back on the machine or had to suction my lungs. After I learned this coughing procedure and could manage to clear my lungs, they felt they could safely remove the tracheotomy and allow the hole in my neck to heal. Because the hole in my neck was larger than normal, it took a while to heal.

What amazed me about the healing process is that they didn't use stitches or anything else to help it along. They simply patched gauze over the hole in my throat until it healed, more than a month later. It was terribly uncomfortable and very un-attractive—just another challenge in my ordeal.

Chapter 24

Need A Little Help

I received many gifts, flowers, and balloons from visitors and I kept them in the corner of the room so I could see them. One night, I woke up with one of the balloons directly in my face, bumping me in the nose. I was staring face to face with a big yellow smiling balloon, and I didn't think it was funny. At the time, I didn't have any movement of my arms so I couldn't reach up and push the balloon away. I tried to blow it away, but I didn't have enough breath. I tried to bite it so it would bust, but I couldn't get my teeth into it. As much as I wanted to move it away, I had no ability to do so. I became so upset that I began to cry, and called for the nurse to come and help.

The nurse put the balloon back in the corner and took my vital signs to make sure everything was okay, then left the room. I closed my wet eyes and fell back to sleep. Thirty minutes later, I awoke with that same balloon in my face again. I immediately started bawling. The reality of paralysis continued to marinate in my mind. I was so upset to know I had no control over this situation. Again I called the nurse and again the nurse rescued me from the persistent, happy faced balloon. I continued to cry. No matter what I did, I couldn't move that balloon.

For some unexplainable reason, my crying turned into laughter. My nurse thought I was becoming hysterical and tried to calm me down. I laughed harder and harder. It soon became infectious, and she began laughing with me. We laughed and laughed at the yellow smiley-faced balloon that wouldn't leave me alone.

Perhaps the balloon wanted to bring me a moment of fun, and teach me a valuable lesson. You can find humor in almost any situation. And, if you are able to find a little humor, you feel a lot better about your situation. Had my situation changed? No. Could I move my arms? No. Did I feel better? Yes, for the moment. I guess my laughter allowed me to let off some steam. I slept much better the rest of the night.

Of course, the nurse tied all of my balloons in a bunch to the back of the chair in the corner. No way was Mr. Smiley getting loose again.

During the often-traumatic rehabilitation process, I was very fortunate to always have certain people with me. I don't know what I would have done without the support of family and friends. My mom, dad, stepfather, brother, sister, and a girl that I had been dating prior to the accident, played a major role in rotating shifts to make sure that I was taken care of. It was imperative for my mental and physical comfort to have someone with me at all times. My problems were not all as benign and amusing as the Mr. Smiley incident.

When your body sustains an injury as big as mine, it is no surprise that many of the body's functions don't work correctly. Because of my injury, my body could no longer regulate its temperature; I had real problems maintaining comfort. At any time, I could go from one extreme to the other. I would get overheated and need to be cooled with cold washcloths and fans blowing on me from different angles. But the next moment, I would be freezing and need to be wrapped in blankets like a cocoon. I've learned that the sudden temperature changes can be life threatening, but with the help of my loved ones, I learned to deal with this aspect of my injury.

In addition to needing help with my body temperature, I

needed someone with me when I was learning to breathe, and when I needed to eat. I physically needed people to help me do certain things, but there was also an emotional need to have someone with me all the time. I am so thankful for all of the love and support I received during that time. My special, familiar faces helped me push on. But pushing on was never easy.

Although my time at Health South was shared by my family and by my special friends, one of the biggest challenges that I faced was loneliness.

At first, I received tons of letters and visits from people saying that they missed me, all promising that they would do anything for me at any time. I looked forward to visiting hours every day at 6:00 p.m. The hype and promise started slowing down after the first few weeks and finally, most of the people stopped coming. I had the same few faithful visitors, who were mainly my family and a few friends. Ironically, the friends who continued to visit weren't the ones that I thought would be coming to visit. I really saw the true colors of some of my closest friends, and it was a major disappointment.

School was getting ready to start and my friends were finishing up their summer jobs and heading back to Radford. I felt like they all forgot about me, and it really hurt. I selfishly thought that because I was injured that everyone else's lives should stop. It was a hard reality for me to grasp; my life had changed, but their lives were going on as normal. I was paralyzed and they were still able-bodied people, getting ready for the semester to start.

During that time, I would look down at my body every day and think, *this is not me! There is no way that this is happening to me.*

Every morning when I woke, I would just lie there wishing that I could get up. I didn't want to believe that life would never be the same. I kept thinking that I was going to get better, that I would wake up from this horrible nightmare.

I would look in the mirror and say to myself, "This is only temporary. I will be able to get up and walk right out of this room any day now! This just has to be a dream…or a nightmare!" To be honest, on certain days and occasions I still look in the mirror and think the same thing.

At first, I was positive and I kept a good attitude. I would grit my teeth and do everything they asked me to do. Then, I would ask them to help me do more. Maybe the loneliness had a lot to do with my behavior. I somehow thought I could will myself better by doing more than I was asked to do and that I could get there faster. I would push myself until I accomplished each tiny goal and bask in the feeling of accomplishment.

Then I became aware that they were only tiny accomplishments and that I wasn't progressing as quickly as I wanted. I started to compare my results with others around me, whose injuries weren't as debilitating as mine.

My friends and family saw the change in me, and became concerned. I started to get depressed and needed a miracle to get back on track. Then something happened that changed everything for me and gave me the direction that I needed to move on.

Chapter 25

My Inspiration

God's love for us is boundless. When I look back now, I can see where He performed one of many miracles in my life.

I was lying in my bed frustrated, crying, and feeling sorry for myself when I was blessed. A man named Robin Clark came into my life. Robin is quadriplegic like I am, and has been injured for over thirty years, due to a diving injury he sustained when he was just sixteen years old. Robin came into Health South one day to work out on the exercise equipment. Some of the staff told him about me and asked him to come and talk to me. They gave him a brief run down of what had happened and told him that I was having a really hard time dealing with everything.

Being a happy-go-lucky guy, he smiled and said, "Sure. I would be glad to meet Chris and give him a little pep talk."

Well, this little old man rolled into my room and gave me a pep talk all right. He told me to get my scrawny little butt out of bed (not in those exact words) and stop feeling sorry for myself.

"I know what you're thinking right now," he explained. "I've been there myself. You're thinking that this isn't happening to you. That life just can't go on like this and you want to quit. I'm telling you right now, THIS IS happening to you and lying there dwelling on it isn't going to change a thing. The faster you get over that, the easier your life is going to be and the faster your life is going to go on."

I don't know about you, but after hearing his statement, I didn't really consider it to be much of a pep talk. Initially, I was pretty angry with this guy! At the same time though, what he said really hit home, because he was the first person to tap into my true thoughts and feelings. He didn't sugarcoat things for me by telling me everything was going to be fine and that I was going to be happy with my situation. He was very honest with me to the point where, as much as I hated listening to him, it did me some good. Robin really knew what I was going through. I guess you can say that it was a love-hate relationship at the beginning. I loved his honesty and the fact that he could empathize with me, but I hated the reality of what he said and the way he said it.

After chatting with him a bit and letting him know that I was going to walk again, he replied smoothly.

"If your goal is to walk again," he said, "how do you expect to reach that goal if you just continue to lie there in bed feeling sorry for yourself? You have to get up and make it happen!"

At that point, I was so mad at him that I asked him to leave the room. As he left, I remember watching him turn the corner with a smile on his face. At that moment, I realized for the first time that my life could go on. To tell you the truth, I hated to see Robin leave that day because I wasn't sure if he would come back after the way I had spoken to him. The following day I realized that I wasn't finished with Robin, and he wasn't finished with me either. Around the same time as the day before he flew around the corner into my room with that same big grin on his face.

"How's it going today, Skinner?" he asked, as if he knew I wanted to see him again.

"Much better," I replied with a half smile. I was genuinely happy to see him.

Our visits together became a daily event that I anticipated with excitement. Robin began visiting every day at around the same time. I really enjoyed seeing him, and listening to all of his stories. He told me all about life in a wheelchair. He explained to me how I could still do most of the things that I used to do, just not in the same way. I listened to his stories about the accomplishments he achieved since his accident changed his life. He told me that he has been in a hunting magazine, that he goes snow skiing, and that he has traveled across the country. These tales gave me hope, and motivation for my future. I thought he was absolutely amazing, and a huge inspiration. I wanted my attitude to be just like his.

I became so comfortable with Robin that I must have asked him over a million questions. It got downright personal sometimes, as I sought solutions to prepare myself for what was to come. He answered every question honestly and without reservation.

One of my biggest concerns was what my life would be like sexually. All my life I had dreamed of having a family and being a good husband and father. I have always loved children and was relieved to find out that I would still be able to have children with the use of certain technology. We talked about that technology, and what relationships would be like for me as a person with a disability. I felt comfortable around him and he felt comfortable around me. He said I reminded him of himself when he was younger. What I loved about Robin was that he never lied about anything. Other people would tell me that I could still be the same person I was before the accident and that nothing would change.

But Robin told me straight up, "No, your life is never going to be the same. No, it's not going to be fun all the time. Yes, you're going to be frustrated and yes, you're going to hate life at times. You're going to be angry and no one can explain it to you. There is no explanation or reason for this."

He also gave me an outlook on life that I will never forget. "Things happen sometimes," he said, "that basically just stink. So what are you going to do about it? What can you do about it? Are you going to lie there in bed and feel sorry for yourself, or are you going to get up, smile, and take things one day and time?"

I made a promise to myself that this was the perspective that I was going to live by. I said to myself, *I am going to focus on the things that I DO have rather than focus on the things that I don't have!*

I know that this concept is easier said than done, but if we can just figure out how to incorporate it into our daily lives, everything could be much more pleasant.

Using the lessons that I learned from Robin, I pressed on, looking for anything positive in my situation. When things got hard, I talked to him and he always helped me see a different perspective.

"Skinner, look at what you have. Look at all this technology. Look at your wheelchair and this bed. You have all this stuff. I didn't have any of this," he would tell me. "I had none of it. It was the Stone Age of medicine for spinal cord injuries when I had mine."

Listening to him talk about how much harder it was to heal physically, with less technology, I began feeling increasingly motivated. I realized that I needed to quit making excuses for myself. Granted, it was still a very tough situation, regardless of the technology. Anytime someone goes through such a life-changing event, the pain is very real. This is why we have to be careful when we minimize another person's pain. We have no idea how another human being is feeling, because we can never actually live in their shoes.

Robin never said things in a way that made me feel as

though he didn't respect the pain that I was going through. If anyone was minimizing pain in others, it was me!

He challenged me indirectly. I thought to myself, *If this old man has gotten to where he is without all this technology, then I have got to do the same and even more. I'm the man, and I'm going to do it.*

I used this man's situations and experiences as my motivation to push harder. I looked at him and realized that I didn't have any excuses. I had no reason to "punk out." I remember having the distinct feeling one gets with a breath of fresh air, suddenly energized.

I repeatedly challenged myself by comparing my accomplishments to his. I'd say, "I bet you weren't doing this much just two months after your accident."

He'd always be amused, and say, "Nope. I was flat on my back for three months."

Those types of humble responses kept me going. I'd tell myself, "I'm doing better than Robin and look at him now. He's living on his own. He's driving. He has a job. He got married. He does anything he wants to do. Good gosh, if I'm doing this in a month, I'll be walking before too long."

I have the utmost respect for Robin Clark. He knew exactly what I was doing when I used his experiences to motivate myself, but he didn't care. What he really wanted more than anything was for me to move on, and be successful. He was and still is my mentor and inspiration. I love him, and we are best friends to this day. Sometimes I think of him as my football coach. When I need a push, he grabs my helmet, bangs heads with me, and then pats me on the butt and tells me to get back in the game. When I'm down, he gets me up, and when I'm up, he keeps me humble. We all need a Robin Clark in our lives.

Chapter 26

Keeping On

Another difficult time I had mentally was during a team meeting with my therapists. They asked me what my goals were. They wanted to know what I wanted out of therapy and what they could do to help. I thought the answer was rather obvious.

"I want to walk again!" I said, boldly.

After what seemed to be an eternity of silence one of the therapists replied.

"Chris I don't mean to sound harsh, but I don't want you to set your goals too high."

I felt a sudden rage come over me. "Don't ask me what my goals are, if you don't want to know," I told them. "I can only set my goals where I want them…and I want to set them high. I want to walk again."

Nothing irritates me more than someone telling me that I am unable to do something. I want to encourage you to set your goals as high as your imagination can go. Always remember that no one can tell you what you can or cannot accomplish. The only person who can keep you from achieving your goals is yourself.

I know that these therapists were not intentionally trying to destroy my hopes. In their minds, they were just trying to be realistic.

But what is "realistic?" How can another person determine what is realistic or unrealistic about your life's aspirations?

It is simple. They can't, as long as you do not allow it. I don't believe that any human being has the knowledge or power to look at another person and say, "You can't" or "You'll never be able to."

I said to myself, *they don't know who I am, or what I am able to accomplish. I don't care what the statistics say! My name is Chris Skinner and I will accomplish my goals.*

If you ever feel down or discouraged, and are not sure if you can succeed, try this method. Say to yourself, "My name is _____, and I will accomplish my goals!" Say it out loud. Say it to everyone who doubts you. Then, give everything you have to try to accomplish that goal, not simply to prove others wrong (although that can feel pretty good), but for yourself.

I remember after I said those things to my therapists they answered, "Umm…Well…Okay, then, but we'll need to set smaller goals to get to the bigger ones." It was an answer I could accept, so we set goals and got started.

I embraced the suggested smaller goals and tried my hardest to do everything the therapists asked of me. Sometimes when we finished with therapy, I stayed and asked to do more. I wanted so badly to make it happen—to walk again! I continued to push myself and give all that I had when attempting each exercise.

Although I was trying to accept things for what they were and go on with my life, I still rode a roller coaster of emotions. I found myself getting frustrated and angry. I was frustrated while I was in therapy and frustrated when I wasn't. The hardest times were when I had nothing to do but sit around and think. At those times, I would break down and cry.

I felt like I was not accepting things—I was just pretending. I didn't know how long I could keep up this happy pretense. I didn't want to accept this. I didn't want to go on with my life this way. I was mad at God, mad at myself, and mad at everyone else.

Even with people like Robin Clark in our lives, we experience the ups and downs of emotions. Things are not always going to run perfectly smooth and according to our plans. I encourage each of us to accept this reality and prepare for it, so that when rocky times occur we are ready to fight against the adversity and win our battles with discouragement much quicker.

Chapter 27

Feeling Sorry For Myself

Often, I felt sorry for myself when I was in the hospital. I complained about my life and the situation that I was now in. I know that you're probably thinking, "Well heck yeah, I would complain too if I were in that situation!"

Some of you reading this could very well be in a situation similar to mine, or worse. I can assure you, however, that each and every one of us has certain areas in our lives in which we struggle in some way and feel pain. We cannot minimize another person's pain compared to our situation, nor can we minimize our own pain compared to that of others.

Sometimes people tell me that they are sorry for complaining about their sprained ankle or hurt knee around me because they assume my situation must be much more painful. The truth of the matter is that pain is pain. Everyone's pain is real to him or herself. Would it be fair for me to call people wimps if they complained about their sprained ankles and hurt knees, just because I can't feel mine? The answer is a big fat "NO." Their pain is just as real as my own.

One day in rehab, I experienced a major wake-up call. I had been telling myself that life was unfair and that I was the unluckiest person on the planet. Just then, I heard a group of people crying down the hallway. Being the nosy, curious person I am, I decided to roll down and peek into the room.

As I turned the corner, I found myself staring face-to-face with a twelve-year-old boy. He was paralyzed from the neck down and confined to a ventilator. He looked terrified. His family circled around him and cried. In that moment, I looked down at my arms and realized how fortunate I was just to be able to move them.

It is imperative that during the course of our lives we remember that there are always people who are dealing with harder circumstances than our own. I know it is easier said than done. At the rehabilitation center, I thought I was the only one going through pain and that it couldn't get any worse. Obviously, that was totally false. There were people right next to me who could only blink their eyes. Can you imagine what they must go through on a daily basis?

That was the first time that I realized that I was being selfish and self-centered. It gave me more motivation because I looked at myself in a completely different way. I thought to myself, *I have my arms, and I can do a lot of things.*

It was really strange being around people in wheelchairs. I had never really noticed handicapped people before. I didn't feel like I belonged with them; I felt like I was different. For the first time in my life I felt like a minority and I didn't like that either. I didn't want it. I thought, *This is not who I am!*

Being considered a disabled person opened my eyes to a whole new world. I noticed things that I had never noticed before. It was like when you buy a new car, one that you had never noticed before, and suddenly you start seeing them everywhere you go. It is not a coincidence; your eyes open to the things that you have in your life.

When I started to realize that I was disabled and one of a minority, it hit me like a ton of bricks. I felt very alone. Even though I knew Robin, and realized that many people before me have been in this situation, I still felt like there was no one else in the world who could possibly understand exactly what I was going through. I became self-absorbed in a way. I was in a situation that I had absolutely no control over. This was the first major thing that I had ever encountered that was unchangeable.

Before the accident if I were to get into trouble, get bad grades, get a speeding ticket, or break my arm, I could fix it. There was always something I could do to change the situation. What was so devastating about dealing with the consequences of drinking and driving was that they were irreversible. "If I could turn back time…" Lyrics from Cher's famous song frequently echoed in my mind. It was funny—I didn't even like Cher's music, but the words fit my thoughts perfectly.

Thousands of people have lost loved ones because of alcohol and drugs. Thousands more have had to deal with situations like mine, due to alcohol and drug use. I hope and pray that you never have to deal with a situation like this. I pray that you pay close attention to my experiences and make each and every one of your decisions wisely. There is no need for our society to continue to suffer when we have the power to change our behavior.

My situation affected my mother just as badly as it affected me, if not more so. I could see in her eyes how helpless she felt, because she couldn't fix what had happened to me. I'm sure you can tell that my mother loves me no matter how much I have messed up, and she is always willing to make sacrifices to help me. But there was no fix to this situation, no matter what sacrifices she made.

I broke my mother's heart when I chose to drink that night and get into that car. My accident changed her life forever. The consequences weren't just my own. They affected the person I loved and who loved me so very much. It was a hard reality to accept.

Being around other people who are going through similar situations gave me a sense of camaraderie. It was like being in a wheelchair qualified me for a wheelchair fraternity. Every time I saw someone in a wheelchair, I automatically felt a strong bond and wanted to talk to him or her. It seemed like no matter how many able-bodied people I talked to about my accident, I couldn't gain satisfaction from our conversation. I would automatically shut them out.

They have absolutely no idea what I am going through.

There is nothing better in life than having someone that you can vent your true feelings to and confide in. So many times when we talk to people about our struggles, they offer us advice. I don't know about you, but when I vent about my situation I am not looking for answers. I just want someone to listen and pat me on the shoulder or give me a hug. I encourage you to find someone in your life that you can express your true emotions to. Explain that you are not seeking answers; you just need a sympathetic ear. It can make a world of difference—trust me.

I met several other people close to my age in wheelchairs at the rehab center. There was a guy named Jason who had been in a dirt biking accident. He was three to four weeks ahead of me in rehab. He was paraplegic, meaning he was paralyzed from the waist down, but had complete use of his upper body and hands. It helped me tremendously to know that Jason was going through a similar situation. Many times we talked and complained about the hardships we experienced on a daily basis, sharing stories and confirming negative feelings. This helped us both let off steam and clear our minds. I tried many times to complain to my mother, but I felt like I was bringing her down. I had already put her through so much. I didn't want to burden her even more.

You've heard the saying, "the grass is greener on the other side." Well, to be perfectly honest with you, being around Jason made it harder for me at times. I often felt jealous and sometimes angry because of his abilities. Because he was a paraplegic, he had full use of his hands and was able to pick up drinks and do many things on his own. His grass was so much greener. Some days I sat in the gym and watched him learn to transfer himself in and out of his wheelchair. It made me feel sick to my stomach.

I remember asking God, "Why couldn't I have been a paraplegic? Why couldn't I have broken my neck just a little bit farther down my spinal cord?"

I often thought about how nice it would be to have just a little bit more mobility. I still catch myself thinking that way.

How much time do we spend comparing ourselves to someone else? If you are like me, the answer is "entirely too much." Our time could be better spent focusing on our own abilities. As hard as it is, we need to remind ourselves that we can make our grass just as green as that other side if we spend more time fertilizing it. We must reach a point when we accept who we are and what we have, and then roll with it. Please do not be discouraged by these words. Believe me, I know that it is a very hard thing to do. We are in control of our own destiny. We have the ability to make our grass as green as we like.

I met another young man named John at rehab. He had a horribly tragic story. He was with a buddy who lost control of a car going 80 mph and hit a telephone pole head on. John was trapped in the car with the dashboard crushed around his legs. The car caught on fire and all he could do was scream for help while he witnessed his own legs being burned severely. When the paramedics arrived, they had to drag him out of the car by grabbing his arms.

In their efforts to save his life, John's hands sustained nerve damage. He didn't have full use of his hands, and his fingers were curled like mine, but he was able to pick things up, feed himself and transfer himself. Unfortunately, his legs were burned so badly in the car accident that he had to have both amputated. During one of our conversations, I expressed to him that I wished I could be in his situation. I wished I could give up my legs and have the use of my hands.

John replied sternly, "No, you don't Skinner. One day when they find the cure for spinal cord injuries, you will be able to use your whole body again with no scars!"

He made me realize that I was fortunate because my body was still mostly in tact. You see? The grass is not always greener. I am not sure where Jason and John are today, but I am thankful for the perspectives that I gained from both of them.

Being around other individuals who had experienced catastrophic life-changing events helped me keep a decent attitude. I am not saying I was happy others were going through such misery, because I hated it for every single one of us. It was important to know I wasn't alone in suffering; it inspired me to drive forward.

I tried to smile as much as possible and push through my daily trials to the best of my ability. I think that, at this point, I still hadn't realized the magnitude and severity of the situation. I didn't believe that it was reality. I eventually realized that it was my reality, and is my reality to this day. This is my life now; I can't go back.

You have heard me emphasize the fact that we can't go backwards in life. The only thing we can do is focus on the here and now. I beg you, wherever you are in life, to realize that you are not invincible. Take a deep breath and be thankful for your life, because it is a gift.

I remember lying on my back counting ceiling tiles and listening to the noises of the hospital, wishing and pleading to go back in time to make a different decision. All I wanted to do was stand up, walk out of that hospital, and forget the whole thing had ever happened. It's too bad that life doesn't work that way.

Wake-up, friends! You have to deal with the consequences of your decisions. Take it from me; you don't want to deal with some types of consequences. Take control of your life now, while you still have the ability, so that you won't have to face trials like mine.

Chapter 28

Back At Home

I finished acute rehab at UVA Health South in mid-August, about two months after my accident. I was sent home and placed on a waiting list for Woodrow Wilson Rehabilitation Center (WWRC). WWRC has been open since the 1940s and provides services for people with disabilities. It is considered one of the top facilities in the state, and arguably, the east coast. The purpose and main goal of the Center is to assist clients to become as independent as possible and to prepare them to be successful in "the outside world."

Before going to WWRC, I was advised to go home for a while to get an idea of what it is like to be a disabled person in my home and community. This allowed me to experience firsthand how things would be in everyday life. During these few weeks at home, I was able to see some areas that I wanted to focus on at WWRC. Looking back now, I wish I had stayed home a little longer so that I could have made a really good list of what I needed to learn and work on. With only three weeks at home, I didn't have a good concept of what real everyday life was all about.

The time I spent at home was a very lonely and depressing for me. The fact that I was disabled really started to sink in. My family didn't have time to renovate their house to make it completely handicapped accessible. We were inexperienced, so we made many mistakes at first. The temporary ramp we built was too steep, and I needed help getting up and down it. The van we purchased was not exactly what I needed, and therefore, was difficult to use. I was sent home with a rented power wheelchair that wasn't a correct fit for me. It was the only one available with a tilt system, which I needed to maintain my skin integrity. It was very old, long, and needed a large turning radius. I was inexperienced at using any wheelchair, let alone this monstrosity.

The inside of the house wasn't very accessible. I was only able to use the living room, kitchen, and dining room, and even that was difficult. I kept running into doorways and walls with my wheelchair as I tried to drive through the space. My parents bought the house only a month before my accident and it was beautiful—white moldings everywhere and sand colored carpets. Every nick or ding I put in the walls felt like it cut into me as well. Every wheel mark on the carpet made me feel horrible and re-emphasized the fact that I was so handicapped now.

We had to use the dining room as my bedroom because I couldn't maneuver the wheelchair down the narrow hallways. We rented a special hospital bed and hung a curtain for privacy. To watch TV with the family, the whole bed was pushed out into the living room. As my mother and step-dad wheeled the bed into place, nearly taking up the entire walking area, I had to keep myself from crying. Just a few months ago, I had visited with them and had sat in this living room and watched TV. I had walked out on the deck and cooked a surprise dinner for them using the gas grill. I had slept in the guest bedroom and had washed dishes at their kitchen sink. It was a huge difference in a very short period of time. The contrast brought me down even further. Needless to say, it definitely wasn't the ideal situation, but we made do with what we had and kept plugging forward.

During the three weeks between rehab centers, school started back at Radford. I thought about all the excitement that a new semester entailed. I missed my friends so much, and couldn't understand why I had stopped receiving phone calls. I couldn't deal with the reality that everyone was going on with their lives and mine had completely stopped. Of course, it hadn't really stopped, but it was definitely on hold while I was "temporarily out of service."

I had been dating a girl off and on for about a year before my accident occurred. Although we had a rocky relationship, we were very close. We even lived together at one point. To be honest, before my accident, I really didn't treat her well. I took her for granted like so many things in my life. After the accident, I was so afraid that I had no chance to continue or pursue a relationship that I latched onto her and tried everything in my power to keep her around.

At first, I never wanted her to leave the hospital. Things went well initially. We both held out hope that I would fully recover. As the days went by and my physical capabilities stayed the same, I could sense her slipping farther and farther away. She began spending less time with me at the hospital. She returned home more often and stayed there longer each time.

Then I noticed that she didn't touch me as much. In the beginning she always held my hand, rubbed my head, or kissed me. She began coming into the room and sitting in a position which felt distant. She stopped kissing me unless I asked her to, and stopped saying I love you unless I said it first. It was such a terrible feeling to lie there, knowing what was happening, unable to do anything to prevent it. I knew that it was ending, but wasn't willing to accept it. I had never in my life experienced the feeling of a girl breaking up with me.

It tore my heart to pieces to talk to her on the phone and hear about all of the fun that was happening at school during those lonely three weeks at home. I wanted so badly to be at school and be the fun-loving fraternity guy I used to be. I wanted so badly to be in control like I used to be. During my second week at home I got a phone call from her and knew by the tone of her voice what was going to happen.

I remember her saying, "I still love you, Skinner, but I just don't think I can handle this situation!"

I don't remember any more of our conversation that night, but I do know that it was very short and to the point. I hung up the phone and gritted my teeth as tears rolled down my cheeks. I was extremely angry, yet I could understand her point of view. I didn't want to deal with the situation either.

After that night, she made a few attempts to call me. Every time we talked, I tried to make her feel as bad as possible. When she told me about the fun things going on in her life, I said, "I can't believe you're having fun. Why aren't you missing me?"

I put such a guilt trip on her. I don't think that I was angry with her as much as I was angry about the situation. I regret the way that I treated her before and after the accident. I am glad that she was there for me for those first two excruciating months. It was a hard situation for two twenty-year-old kids to go through.

A valuable lesson that I learned from this situation is that sometimes there are people who will only be in our lives for a season, or for a reason. During that time, we need to treat these individuals with respect. I don't know about you, but I do not like having enemies and I do not like confrontation. Life is too short and precious. I am choosing to look for the positives in all of my past and future relationships, and I encourage you to do the same.

I know that some of you have been severely hurt by someone and are probably thinking there is no way you can find anything positive in that relationship. I can understand that, but maybe you can find a positive in yourself that came out of that relationship. I used my pain and anger to motivate myself to return to college. I could easily look back and get angry with my ex-girlfriend if I really wanted to. Would it be fair though? I didn't treat her well in the first place, and she gave up most of her summer and a great job working at Camden Yards in Baltimore, MD to sit in a little hospital room and learn how to take care of me. I guess it all comes down to the Golden Rule we learned in grade school, "Treat others the way that you want to be treated!"

Chapter 29

Hope Spelled "WWRC"

Three weeks at home finally came to an end and it was time to move on to what would be my new home for the next two months. I remember being so excited about going to Woodrow Wilson, because of all the great things that I had heard about it. An acquaintance from my hometown who had been injured in an automobile accident went to WWRC and came back with twice as much movement and independence. Another young man from my hometown who became paralyzed after a diving accident went there and ended up walking again. These were the stories I heard about Woodrow Wilson, and this was the reality that I wanted for myself.

I remember the first day that I arrived at Woodrow Wilson. It was a Sunday evening, which of course was not a workday for most employees at Woodrow. The nursing staff and aides were the only people at the facility besides the clients. I started feeling that same nervous and scared feeling that comes on me when I have to deal with change. I was completely blindsided when the nursing staff took me to my room and I discovered I wasn't just going to have one roommate, I was going to have three. All of the rooms at Woodrow Wilson consisted of four patients per room. Now keep in mind that up to this point, I have always stayed in a private room, and my family and friends were allowed to stay with me.

I remember asking one of the nurses, "Where will my mom be able to sleep?"

The nurse looked at me and replied, "At this facility we are geared toward helping clients gain independence, therefore friends and family are not permitted to stay in the room with you."

She went on, saying, "There are apartments that your parents are permitted to stay in if you want; but don't worry, we will take good care you."

Instantly, I looked in the direction of my mother to see her reaction. I guess I was hoping deep down inside that she was going to fight the system like she had done before and find a way for me to get my own room. We had been told prior to coming to Woodrow Wilson that this was the way things were. I guess it didn't really hit home until that moment. It might sound a little melodramatic to you, but this was a very emotional time for me. I almost felt like I was saying goodbye to my parents forever. Another major change was about to occur and I wasn't sure if I could handle it.

I had become so dependent on my parents that I was devastated with the thought of them being three and one-half hours away from me. If my stepfather hadn't sped up the unpacking process and got my mom out of Dodge before I realized what was going on, I don't know if I would have stayed at Woodrow at all. I probably would have freaked out like before and demanded her to stay. Even being as exhausted and emotional as I was, I spent practically the entire night lying on my back looking at the ceiling. I thought about all that had gone on in the past three months and everything that was about to take place. I was frightened and unsure about where I was and what my future entailed.

The next morning I had my intake meeting. I was familiar with this type of meeting. It was very similar to the meetings I had during my stay at Health South. I knew that they were going to ask me what my goals were and how they could help me achieve them. I rolled into the meeting trying to keep my head high and exude as much confidence and determination as possible. After everyone was seated, the staff began going around the table introducing themselves. They told me their names and job titles followed by what their specific roles were going to be in my rehabilitation. I was excited to meet my physical therapist and occupational therapist. As luck would have it, they happened to be attractive young women. God definitely knew what He was doing as far as keeping me motivated.

One of the facilitators of the meeting turned to me and asked politely, "Chris, what can we do for you here at Woodrow Wilson? What are your personal goals?"

I knew that my ultimate goal was to walk again, but remembering the words of wisdom that Robin had given me I realized that I had to take one day at a time. There were more immediate issues that needed to be addressed in order for me to become as independent as possible. I explained to my new occupational therapist that I was planning to return to Radford University and would be living on my own. We discussed some things that I needed to work on that would help me be as independent as possible in a university setting.

Still using Robin's situation as a driving force of motivation, I explained to my new physical therapist that I wanted to be able to transfer myself, which means to pick up my body and put myself into my wheelchair, without assistance. Starting off, I explained to her that I at least wanted to learn how to do pressure releases so that I could be in a wheelchair that didn't have a tilt system. I was very unhappy at the time with the wheelchair that I was using. Bless her heart; I really gave my physical therapist a hard time about my wheelchair and my desire to do pressure releases. It wasn't anything against her personally, I was just fired up and wanted to have some kind of control over my own my own body and my situation.

I know some of this talk might sound foreign to you so let me explain. When someone is paralyzed, it is necessary to consistently perform something called a pressure release in order to prevent pressure sores. A pressure release is exactly what it sounds like; it is taking the pressure off of a certain area for a certain length of time. Here is a quick anatomy lesson for you. All of us have two butt bones—a right tuberosity and a left tuberosity. If anyone of us were to sit on them long enough, preventing blood to flow to the area, those bones would eventually penetrate your tissue and puncture your skin leaving a wound called a pressure sore. When you are sitting in a chair and feel uncomfortable, you automatically shift your weight from side to side or just stand up. The brain sent you a message to protect the skin in that area and you made the necessary adjustments for the blood flow to return to the area. All this happens automatically because you can feel sensations. You probably don't even notice that you are shifting.

For someone like me who is paralyzed and unable to feel the uncomfortable sensations, I am very susceptible to getting pressure sores. Some people in my situation are able to train themselves to move side to side frequently to prevent them. Because of the severity of my injury, I was unable to do this, and therefore, needed a wheelchair with a tilt system. The tilt system allows a person in my condition to tilt back to about a forty-five degree angle and take the pressure off of the tuberosities. I was told that I would have to tilt back once every thirty minutes for at least two to five minutes. I absolutely didn't want a wheelchair like that. First of all, because of the hydraulics of this chair, it was taller than a normal chair. Before my accident I was six foot, one inch and had a long torso. All this added together made me really tall in the wheelchair, which caused all kinds of problems for me. This made it impossible to find a van that I could get in and out of without bumping the top of my head. I could never find a table that my wheelchair would fit under so I could eat a normal meal with family or friends. Second, I thought it made me look more handicapped because of the headrest, which is necessary when you tilt back. Wheelchairs with tilt systems all looked basically alike. To make things worse, they all reminded me of an old, oversized Cadillac.

Similar to Health South, Woodrow Wilson reminded me of basic training. I had nurses and aides coming into the room, turning on the lights and waking me up early every morning. I hardly ever felt like I had any privacy and there were rules that all patients had to abide by. Sometimes I felt like a little kid at a day care center. I understand why they have the rules that they do, but it was difficult to adjust to them after being on my own for so long. I know some of you can understand by just looking at your own life and realizing how set in your ways you are. Just imagine having to move in with your parents, another person, or let's just say a nursing home. It would definitely take a toll on you mentally and would be extremely hard to accept.

After I woke up and got out of bed, I had a certain schedule to followed throughout the day. In the morning, I would have one hour of physical therapy, and then one hour of occupational therapy. After lunch, I would have one hour of recreational therapy, which I really enjoyed.

The most popular activity at the center was painting ceramics. At first, I made fun of ceramic painting, but I soon got hooked. I actually had a great time with ceramics, and even agreed to use adaptive equipment to help me paint. Painting during recreational therapy was a breakthrough for me and played a major role in helping me realize that it was okay for me to use adaptive equipment in order to accomplish tasks.

In the afternoon, I had another hour of physical therapy and another hour of occupational therapy. That was basically a full day of work for me. I always looked forward to these sessions and the hard work. One reason I enjoyed working hard was the fact that it took my mind off my problems and forced me to be positive. The other reason was I really enjoyed the staff that worked at Woodrow Wilson. They always seemed to have a very upbeat, positive attitude and when it was your time for therapy, they would give you all they had in order to help you achieve your goals.

My physical therapist, Suzie Jefferis, was and is one of the most amazing people I have ever met. She is about five foot, four inches and has short, dirty blond hair. Her eyes are as green as a four-leaf clover and, full of compassion. From the beginning of therapy, I felt as if she were a little angel sent just for me. She was very professional and organized, but at the same time very caring and sincere. Unfortunately, I know that I was one of the most difficult patients, if not the most difficult, she ever had to deal with. I had such high expectations coming into Woodrow Wilson, and was constantly complaining about my progress, and comparing myself to other individuals who had been through rehab there.

I remember one specific day when I got so frustrated that I basically released all my feelings onto her by saying, "I can't believe that I haven't gotten any better physically! I thought that this place was going to help me regain all kinds of independence!"

After I said that, I remember looking into her eyes and seeing great big puddles of tears forming. She answered me quietly.

"I am doing the best I can do, Chris."

She continued working hard that session and then walked away slowly after we were done for the day. I couldn't tell for sure, but it looked as if she started crying as she turned the corner and went into her office. I know that I wasn't angry with her, I was just angry about my situation.

I can't imagine how many times this must happen at Woodrow Wilson, or any rehabilitation center for that matter, to the therapists. They probably have patients who are angry at their situations and come in with the same type of expectations that I had, and who project all that anger toward their therapist. I can only begin to imagine how tough that must be for them. Day in and day out, they are trying to help individuals achieve their highest potential and their patients, like myself, end up dumping anger and hostility on them. I have so much respect for therapists and all that they do. The truth of the matter is that being with the therapists during the day was what motivated me, kept me going, and gave me something to look forward to each day.

Suzie and I spent our two hours of therapy each day trying to reach my main goal of doing a full pressure release independently. I usually came into the gym and worked out for the first twenty to thirty minutes of therapy on my upper body using special equipment that was adaptable to people with my level of disability. Then we would spend the remainder of our time working on sitting balance and trying to relieve pressure by using the muscles that I still had use of which were my biceps, deltoids, and traps. In the afternoon session, we dedicated the full hour trying any and every possible way we could think of to get the pressure off my tuberosities.

At the rehab center, they used an electronic device called a pressure map which could actually read and project on a computer screen just how much pressure was being exerted in the areas being evaluated. It looked a lot like a weather map because of all the colors used to indicate the levels of pressure being exerted. It ranged from very light green (meaning that there was very little pressure), to yellow, to orange and then to dark red (meaning that there was a tremendous amount of pressure on the area). After trying out several different methods of shifting my body along with various cushions to sit on, I was hit with the hard cold fact that I was going to have to order a wheelchair with the tilt system. No matter what method or cushion we tried I was unable to sustain any type of consistent pressure release from my butt bones. Even with the undeniable facts right in front of my face, I still tried to fight by suggesting that the machine was wrong and or I just needed a little bit more time to work on it.

The results of this test crushed me, bringing down my spirit and my morale. I didn't believe in limitations up to this point and still have a hard time believing in them to this day.

Someone said to me, "Come on, Skinner, think about it in sports terms. If you are five foot tall, then it is improbable that you will pursue a career as a NBA basketball player!"

When I heard this all I could think was, *Yeah, well how about telling that to Spudd Webb and Mugsy Bogues!* These were two players in the NBA who stood right around five feet tall. Spudd Webb even won the NBA slam-dunk competition, for crying out loud!

I wasn't happy that I had to accept a wheelchair that tilted, but I understood that at this point in my rehab, I had to order one. Insurance companies will only allow you to rent one for so long and then you have to purchase one. As far as insurance goes, the tilt chair was the only thing justifiable.

Suzie was great when dealing with my determined attitude as she always encouraged me, never putting down my goals and dreams. We continued with rehab just like this for a couple more weeks until I became unexpectedly ill and had to leave the program early. I was forced to leave due to an infection in my bladder called Mercer. It was discovered on a night that I consider one of my most miserable nights as a quadriplegic.

Remember how I mentioned that during the day at Woodrow Wilson, while I was at therapy, I remained motivated and enjoyed my time with the staff? Well, when five o'clock came around and it was time for the therapists to go home, it was a completely different scenario. The quiet sound of loneliness reminded me of basic training, only worse. Evenings and weekends at Woodrow Wilson would, in my opinion, bring anyone down. There was one room with a pool table and a TV for everyone to share for their entertainment. We were all in wheelchairs and dealing with our own mental battles. It was really tough trying to remain positive in this type of atmosphere. There was just way too much time to think! Almost every night, I would go into my room face the wall next to my bed, and just let out pent up emotions by sobbing and crying to myself. I could eventually calm myself down by focusing on the next day of therapy or look forward to Thursday night outings.

The Thursday night outings were such a blessing. Two or three of the therapists would plan a trip each week and take whoever wanted to go with them out on the town. There was a sign up sheet that was set out every week and you'd better believe my name was on it every single week. We never really went anywhere you would consider extravagant or exciting, but it didn't matter to me as long as I got to get away from the rehab center for a couple hours. We basically would go to the bookstore, Wal-Mart, the mall, a restaurant, or the movies, which I know seem like pretty ordinary, regular trips. Trust me when I say that it felt like we were going to a theme park, or something even better.

At night, once you were put in bed, you were basically on your own. We each had a nursing button we could push in order to get assistance. For people with upper body function who were able to get in and out of bed on their own, this probably wasn't much of a problem for them. In my situation, without the use of my upper body, it was absolutely miserable. Once I was put into the bed, I wasn't able to move again, not even side-to-side, until the morning when I was dressed and put back into my wheelchair. Can you imagine being in a strange place, with the silence of loneliness around you, lying in a bed and not being able to take care of yourself whatsoever? You would have to rely on complete strangers to do their jobs right and take care of you, right?

One night, I was lying in my bed when I started to feel sick and tight all over my body. It felt like my entire body started going through convulsions. I started to get hot and flushed in the face and I began to panic, thinking that I was beginning to have a heart attack. I moved my hand and hit the nurse call button to ask for help. Someone answered the call and asked me what I needed through the intercom.

I said as calmly and politely as possible,

"I think something is wrong with me! I'm feeling very bad!"

She said she would send my assigned nurse right in. A few minutes later, my nurse for this particular shift came into the room and said,

"Okay, what's going on with you?"

Still trying to remain calm I answered,

"I think something is really wrong with me. My whole body feels like it is in a vise and someone keeps tightening it. My face feels flushed and I feel like I might be having a heart attack!"

She stared at me for a moment and then after a short pause, she turned to walk away and said,

"Let's get you some water."

When she returned to the room, she placed the water in my bed near my mouth and told me to calm down and sip slowly on the water. Then she turned around and left the room! I was so shocked that all she did was give me water and then turn around and walk away that I immediately rang the nurse call button again.

The same voice answered the call and asked,

"Can I help you?"

Unable to remain calm, I raised my voice.

"Yes, I feel like I am having a heart attack and I need some medicine or something that will help!"

Again she said she would send my nurse right in. I was getting more and more agitated while I waited for my nurse. I was lying in the bed feeling like I was going to explode and there was no one around who could help me, or even acted like they wanted to help me. It was one of the worst feelings I have ever felt. After a couple minutes went by and no one showed up in my room, I reached down and hit the nurse button again. I was really starting to panic now.

This time without even asking, "can I help you," the same voice said,

"Your nurse will be with you as soon as she can," and then cut me off without allowing me to say anything.

As you can imagine, I really started to get fired up and even more panicked at this point, so I reached down and hit the nurse call button again. All I wanted was someone to come in the room take my vital signs, talk to me for a at least a minute, and give me medicine or something to help relieve the pain that I was feeling.

When you push the nurse call button, it makes a ringing noise at the nurse's station and a light blinks at your bed so you know it is functioning. All of a sudden, I heard the ringing noise stop, and when I looked down, I noticed that my nursing light was off. Thinking that someone accidentally turned off my ringer, I immediately reached down and hit the button again. Once again, I heard the ringing and saw my light blinking, but no one answered the call. After a few seconds passed, the ringing stopped and my nurse call light went off again. I was outraged at this point and began considering a call to my mother to ask her to come and get me.

My nurse finally came into the room and said with a sarcastic sounding voice, "Yes, Mr. Skinner, what can I do for you!"

Holding nothing back at this point I asked, "Why was my nurse button cut off?"

"I was on my way in here and they told you that," she replied defensively.

"I am feeling horrible and I need someone to help me right away!" I retorted angrily. "I need to be checked out and given some sort of medicine to help me feel better. I am beginning to feel even worse than before!" I continued. I started to cry and tighten up even more.

At that point, my nurse did something that completely shocked me and put me over the edge.

"Mr. Skinner, you are just having an anxiety attack and you need to calm down. You are not going to have people snowballing you for the rest of you life!"

I wasn't sure what she meant. I had never heard that term used before, but I assumed by her tone of voice and the way she spoke to me that she was insinuating I was spoiled and expected special treatment. I was always very friendly with the nurses and aides, and, therefore, I was fortunate enough to receive a good amount of attention and care until up to this point. Once more she told me that I just needed to calm down and then she turned around and walked away, but this time she took the nurse call button with her. Can you believe this really happened? Sometimes when I think about it, I still get very angry. It makes me so mad, I think about calling the center to complain even more.

Without wasting any more time, I used the device I had to enable me access to the telephone. I knew my parents were at least three and one-half hours away, so I immediately called

911 for help. I can't believe that I had to call 911 about a medical issue when there were nurses down the hall.

The 911 dispatcher couldn't believe it either. When the dispatcher answered the phone, I started telling the woman all of the symptoms that I was experiencing. Interrupting me, she asked me where I was calling from—they needed an address to dispatch a unit. I told her I was calling from Woodrow Wilson Rehabilitation Center. There was dead silence on the line as she stopped talking for a moment to collect her thoughts.

She then asked me with disbelief, "Sir, are there nurses there that can assist you?"

I quickly answered, "Yes ma'am there are, but they are not helping me and I am starting to feel worse! They removed my call button and I'm unable to get their attention."

After a slight pause she replied, "We will be right there, sir!"

After hanging the phone up, I felt a little sense of ease. I knew help was on the way. The 911 operator must have called back to Woodrow Wilson to talk to the nurses on duty, because less than five minutes later my nurse came back into the room.

"Why did you call 911? They can't do anything more for you than we can at this point."

I replied boldly, "That is the point. You aren't doing anything for me, so at least they will do something!"

She didn't say much more to me that night. I lay and waited for the ambulance to come and pick me up. Eventually, I was taken by ambulance to a local hospital, by myself. Shortly afterward, my father arrived at the hospital to be with me. He lived closer to me than my mother and stepfather. I was very relieved to have him there with me.

Upon arrival, I explained to the doctor what type of pain I was going through. I pleaded and begged him to give me anything to help with the pain. Judging by the doctor's mannerisms and reaction toward me, I could tell he recognized the sincerity in my voice and the pain in my eyes.

He responded quickly, saying, "Sure thing. We will see what we can do right away!"

I lay there in the hospital bed all night with my dad by my side as they ran several different tests on me. True to his word, the doctor did give me something to ease my pain. By the next morning, they decided to send me to UVA Medical Center in Charlottesville, VA where the doctors experienced in my care could assess my situation.

At UVA, I was informed that I had an infection called Mercer and they began an eradication treatment program of antibiotics. I would have to go home for several weeks and follow this program until I could get rid of the infection. I wasn't able to return to Woodrow Wilson Rehabilitation Center until I was well. As it turns out, WWRC was where I contracted this infection. One of my roommates had it when he checked into the center and was sent home as soon as the staff became aware of it. Apparently, because we all shared a bathroom, it wasn't quick enough to prevent my infection in my weakened state. My rehab program was cut short by about six weeks.

Chapter 30

Home Again, Home Again

It was very devastating to have to leave Woodrow Wilson in this manner. I was also upset that I wasn't going to be able to see the therapists anymore, even to say goodbye. I knew there was still more work to do to finish my rehab. It was a major backslide for my morale. I was also so angry with that awful nurse that I wasn't sure if I would ever allow myself to return to that situation again.

In three weeks, I was completely clear of the Mercer. The treatment, although very intensive, had been successful. I had to take a bath everyday, using a special antibiotic scrub. My poor mother had to wash all my clothes, towels, and sheets everyday in hot water, swab my nose several times daily and give me antibiotics on a strict schedule. Everyone in the house had to follow the same routine and we all had to be tested at the end of the three weeks. We were all glad when the three weeks ended and we got back the normal results.

It was mid-November and with the holidays ahead of us, I decided that I did not want to return to Woodrow Wilson Rehab. I instead made the decision to use my time by focusing on my return to Radford University in January. We set up physical therapy and occupational therapy appointments at the local hospital. They were thrilled to get the experience of working with a quadriplegic. We were thrilled that they had the enthusiasm and knowledge from their training to continue my rehab, at least to some degree.

I used the next several weeks to prepare myself physically and mentally for college, as well as to enjoy a little down time at home with family and friends. I remember one of the things my mother and I did was to go over to the mall to get me used to being out in public again. We shopped for Christmas presents and bought items that I needed or just wanted. My mother thought anything was worth the effort or expense, if it lifted my spirits. However, going out in public didn't exactly lift my spirits.

The trips were sheer torture for me. As soon as we pulled into a parking space, I began dreading my decision to come. When the van doors opened, I scanned the parking lot for people passing by. I hoped that I wouldn't see anybody I knew, so I could get out of the van without being observed. I hated the looks on their faces when they saw me. The look was always shock and then discomfort. Sometimes, I could see pity. I hated that one the most.

The moment we walked into the mall, the noise and activity around me started pressing in on me. It was the Christmas season and people were bustling about. I remembered the past year when my mother and I came to this very same mall and I received stares of appreciation from women and girls. People were walking away from me now with uncomfortable looks on their faces. The comparison made me very uncomfortable. I wanted to cry. As we moved further into the mall, I felt worse and worse. Sometimes, we didn't even make it to our intended destination before I would feel like I wasn't able to endure another second.

"Mom, I have to go now. I don't feel well. " And we would leave.

I continued to try and we made many trips to the mall. My sister began taking me and we started meeting our dad for lunch at the food court in the mall. Each time, it became a little easier and I was able to stay a little longer.

Once, my mother was walking with me and I was upset by the reaction of someone passing by. This time I decided to talk to her about it and we stopped for a moment.

"Mom. This is so hard. I hate the way people look at me and I hate what they are thinking about me." I said.

"How do you know what they are thinking?" She asked. "They may have never seen anyone in a wheelchair before and don't know what to say or do. You may be the one who could teach them."

"Well, what am I supposed to do? I hate the look of pity."

"Chris, why don't you just smile? Give them one of those Chris Skinner smiles and say, 'Hi, how are ya?' Be yourself and see what reactions you get then. You are Chris Skinner, fun-loving, and happy guy. Remember who you are and that is who they will see!"

I tried that approach and was grateful that it worked. But when I left the mall, I felt so tired because I was just performing. I wasn't Chris Skinner, happy, fun-loving guy. I didn't know me any more, and I sure didn't like the new version of me.

Chapter 31

Back-To-School Training

After leaving rehab, my mind was set to return to Radford University and complete the degree that I started in 1997. It was only six months since my accident and I had left rehab without completing the program. Everyone repeatedly warned me, it seemed, that I was setting myself up for failure and being too aggressive. Although I knew they were concerned about my physical and emotional well being, I felt again as if my goals were being shot down. It made me furious.

All of the questioning and wondering whether or not I would be able to succeed drove me to be more and more determined and confident. I didn't care what anyone had to say; I was going to make it work. I was, and still am a person who always loves challenges. My mom encouraged me by buying a poster and hanging it on my wall. It had a quote from George Bernard Shaw that said, "The people who get on in this world are the people who look for circumstances they want, and, if they can't find them, MAKE THEM."

Even with my determination, school was without question, and to this day still is, one of the biggest challenges I have ever faced in my life. I'm pretty sure that all of you would agree that life is very challenging at times. The most important thing that we need to remember is that the only person who can keep us from accomplishing our goals, dreams, and aspirations is ourselves. If we have our heart, mind, and soul set on a specific goal, as far as I'm concerned, there is no one on the planet who can stop us from achieving it. However, we must keep in mind that sometimes it takes an incredible amount of patience, effort, and faith to reach those goals of ours.

You see, good things take time. Remember that in your efforts to accomplish your dreams that you must take things one day at a time. You can't turn back time nor can you fast forward to the future; the only thing you can control is the present. It might sound strange or even scary to you at first, but in all actuality it really isn't. The fact is, you have the ability to control what will happen in your future. What an awesome thought! You can have a clean slate at any time, allowing you to focus on the present and look forward to your future.

I had so much to do to get ready. Physically, my body was still in shock. It had functioned a certain way for twenty-one years and now things were completely different. I lost over fifty pounds in four months. I was having a hard time sitting in my wheelchair for more than fifteen minutes without feeling exhausted, dizzy, and nauseous. I was taking several medications a day, which irritated the lining of my stomach and caused severe cases of diarrhea. Some days were worse than others. I often wondered if the sick feelings would ever go away. I wondered if I would ever have a day in which I felt in control and like my old self again.

Despite these challenges, I continued to drive on and focus on my goal of returning to Radford University and completing my degree. I could have easily gone to a different school, maybe even a community college nearby until I built enough strength and confidence to return to Radford. In fact, that is exactly what I was urged to do, but deep down inside I felt a calling to go back to Radford. With that in my mind and in my heart, I began focusing on the future by preparing my body for the adversity to come. I believe that our heart is the highway to our dreams. As long as you are following your heart and feel passionate about what you are doing, you can't go wrong.

I started training my body like a boxer training for a fight. I would pretend I was sitting in class and see how long I could sit without asking for help. I was convinced that I would continue to build endurance and strength so that by the time I got to school and was expected to be in class for a full hour, I would be able to. In the beginning, I was struggling to make it twenty minutes by myself. It was very discouraging and emotionally draining, but I kept on with the training process. Time was running short and I still wasn't able to sit by myself for a full hour.

Another very difficult task I had to overcome was training my bowels and bladder. You must keep in mind I am completely dependent on others to help me use the bathroom. This alone was a dagger in my heart. I had to think about exposing myself over and over again to complete strangers just to survive. All modesty is thrown out the door when you are forced to lie naked in front of several different people. It is, take my word for it, an uncomfortable feeling. The thought of having to do this for the rest of my life was overwhelmingly exhausting and sometimes almost unbearable. I was terrified, and at times didn't want to go on with my goals because of this. Ultimately, when it came down to facing my fears or giving up, I was willing to do what ever it took to succeed.

In rehab I was taught the importance of keeping my bathroom routines on a regular, consistent basis to help cut down on the amount of accidents. When I say accidents, I am talking about urinating or having a bowel movement in my pants without any control or warning. It sounds terrible, but believe me, it is worse than terrible when it actually happens. This is a nightmare for quadriplegics, especially when there's no one to help you clean up afterwards, and you are forced to just sit there and deal with it. Words cannot begin to describe how incredibly helpless you feel as you sit in your chair, knowing you are wet all over with the smell of bowel and/or urine lingering in the air. I never imagined in a million years while I was growing up that I would one day have to wear adult diapers or deal with these situations. When these accidents happen, I can't help but think of the night of June 10, 2000 and what things I could have done differently to avoid this situation today.

So in the training of my bowels and bladder, I had to keep in mind a schedule that would work to accommodate my caretakers' schedules at college. I assumed that my caretakers would be friends or nurses who were also students. This meant that the best time to plan for the process of clearing my bowels, or in other words my bowel program (BP), would be later in the evenings, since most college students do not enjoy getting up early in the morning. Per the recommendations of the rehab physicians, it needed to be done at least every other day. In one way this was good because it meant I didn't necessarily have to find someone for a BP every night. Unfortunately, because I only took showers on the days of BP's, it limited me to about three or four showers a week.

Taking showers is one of my favorite things to do and I hate the fact that I can't just take one whenever I want, for as long as I want. When I sit under the water, lean my head against the wall and close my eyes, I can almost imagine myself normal again. It transports me back in time to a place where it was just me, standing in the shower all alone and whole again. I want to keep the moment ongoing for as long as I can. But, when you are dependent on others and you have to pay them for the time they are there to help, you can't just sit there under the water and relax.

The training and maintenance of my bowels and bladder was and is more dynamic and tricky than putting together a ten thousand piece puzzle of grass. I couldn't empty my bladder on my own, and it needed to be emptied every five hours by means of manual catheterization. This meant that I would have to train several people how to catheterize me for safety and survival. The thought of having to find someone every five hours, every single day and night, over and over again, without my family or any responsible adults around was painful and horrifying. Again, my attitude was that if it needed to be done, so be it. I worked out a schedule of the people who were helping me and impressed upon them the importance to my health that we meet at the appointed time. I am happy to say that the majority of the time, those who committed themselves to being my caretakers were faithful in their responsibilities. There were few occasions when someone was late or didn't show up. At those times, I was able to find someone to step in and help.

After working hard to prepare myself physically, the next step was to make a visit to the campus of Radford University and prepare academically. My mother made several phone calls and set up meetings with faculty and the Disability Resources Coordinator. After obtaining the information of all the people, places, and times, we were finally ready for our trip.

It was during the first week of December 2000. The weather was extremely cold. When we stopped for gas, I remember gazing out the window of the van anxiously. I watched everyone's breath escape from their mouths like clouds of smoke. We drove down I-81, and I began to get butterflies in my stomach as we got closer and closer to Radford. As we pulled off onto Exit 109, I felt almost the same feeling I felt the first time I took the exit some two and one-half years before, except this time I didn't want my parents to just drop me off and go.

We pulled up to Tyler Hall, which was where the disability resources office was, for our first meeting. My stomach suddenly tightened up. It felt as if my insides were being slowly pulled out of me. I was so nervous and it became hard for me to breathe. My mother and I both got out of the van quietly and proceeded down the covered walkway toward the door. Neither one of us said a word as we walked into the building. She put her hand on my shoulder, patting in a reassuring way. I looked up at her and noticed how tense she looked. The forced smile she gave me told me that she was probably feeling very similar to the way I was feeling. We went down the hall, found the office, and were escorted in to meet with the Disability Resources Coordinator, Maureen Weyer.

Mrs. Weyer was a soft-spoken woman with short brown hair. From the beginning, she seemed like a very nice lady who loved her work. She began talking to my mother about setting things up for me to come back to school. I sat quietly looking into her eyes, trying to analyze what she was thinking about the whole situation. It seemed at first that she, too, felt somewhat concerned about my plans to return. Apparently, there had been disabled students in the past that had needed less assistance than I did who were unable to succeed.

Not to mention the fact that she was staring at the transcripts that had my cumulative GPA at Radford University before my accident. The whopping 1.142 had to have been jumping off the page and literally leaping into her mind, causing just a little bit of concern. She must have been thinking something along the lines of,

"How does this kid expect to get by now, in this situation? It is going to be so much harder for him now that he is depending on so many people for his survival, let alone maintaining his class work and grades," followed by the incredulous thought, "He couldn't even come close to getting by when he was able-bodied."

I can only imagine what was going through her mind that day because she never gave us a clue. That's what I would have been thinking. Regardless of her thoughts or feelings, Mrs. Weyer was never discouraging in any way. In fact, what I do remember and respect is that even after having all of those horrible variables in hand, she was still very supportive.

During the meeting with Mrs. Weyer, I signed up for classes and then toured the campus to make sure everything was accessible for me. If I was unable to get in certain classes, due to the fact that they weren't handicap accessible, the University was very accommodating. Radford is a fairly old school and there were some buildings I was unable to access. If I chose a class that was scheduled to be held in a building that I couldn't get into, the University moved the location of that class to another classroom or building that met my needs. This made me feel comfortable and supported.

We had pre-arranged a meeting with the Woodrow Wilson Rehab Occupational Therapist and my DRS counselor to meet with us to look over the dorm room and make recommendations. There were several modifications necessary to ensure my safety and comfort. I needed an automatic door opener with controller from my wheelchair for my individual dorm room and for the handicapped entrance door to the building. The bathroom needed to be modified to accommodate my need for a roll-in shower. I asked for a privacy curtain to pull across the room so my nakedness wouldn't be exposed to hall traffic. I needed individual heating and cooling controls for my room. I had to be able to heat and cool my room at will. I needed permission (and a bed) to allow an attendant to sleep over in my room. This was tricky because the majority of my attendants were female. I needed permission to purchase and install a hospital type bed for myself. They approved the list of modifications and RU maintenance was given their orders. These needed to be completed within four weeks, one of which was a holiday for the University. Time was of the essence.

After our meetings, we had the remainder of the day to work on finding caretakers for the semester. Our initial thought was that we could ask the nursing students at Radford University for help. Radford University is known for its outstanding nursing program. So we asked Mrs. Weyer for suggestions on how to go about doing this hoping that she might have had someone experience something similar to this before. She informed us that Radford University could not provide nursing students as assistants because of liability. This was definitely a bummer, especially since we had been banking on the fact that we would be able to use them, but it didn't stop our pursuit. Sometimes in life when things don't pan out the way that you expect them to, you must remember to just shrug your shoulders and my good friend Robin would say, "keep on keeping on!"

You've probably heard the phrase, "If at first you don't succeed, try, try again!" Not being deterred, my mother followed up by asking if we could hang fliers around campus advertising for help by giving the situation, listing a summary of duties, and stating what type of people we were searching for. After getting approval to hang fliers, she also thought of placing an ad in the local newspaper, and making dozens of calls to agencies and helpers across the county. With all that being done, we drove home content, feeling good about our efforts. The whole ride home I sat in silence hoping that things would work out and people would be interested in helping.

Amazingly, within 48 hours we were receiving phone calls from all sorts of people. There were calls from agencies, people in the county, churches, friends, and also complete strangers. After discussing fees and other terms on a telephone interview, we selected four young ladies that were students at Radford University. Emilee, a junior nursing student, Tracy, a sophomore nursing student, Annie, a sophomore nursing student, and Vanessa, a senior education major.

I was a big brother to a sorority at the time of my accident, so some of those girls played a major role in supporting my return to school as well. Maureen, a sister in the sorority, took charge and organized enormous amounts of support for me. She was constantly calling my mother and me, volunteering assistance in any way. She was great!

It seemed like things were falling into place perfectly. I was all set and prepared for the challenge. My mother and I had all of my classes, paperwork, care, and support ready to go. I honestly thought I was ready to go, until I experienced a mental breakdown. I just started listening to all of those little negative voices inside of my head. I remembered all of the people who told me that I couldn't do this or couldn't do that, and I began to let it affect me. I started panicking, which led me to think that there was no way I could go through with it. Even though things were thoroughly planned out and ready to go, I knew there was no way I could have prepared myself mentally for what I would face. So many terrible thoughts were running through my mind.

I totally lost my positive attitude, and at one point, even decided that I was not going to return to school. I know for a fact that I wouldn't have returned to school and be where I am today if it weren't for the sacrifice my younger sister, Tammy made that Christmas holiday. In spite of a past of being overlooked and treated unfairly, by me in particular, she stepped up voluntarily and unselfishly. We were talking one day and I was explaining to her all of my negative emotions and fears in regard to returning to school. After listening to me, she asked if there was anything she could do to help me achieve my goals. She went on to say that she would be willing to come to Radford with me until I felt comfortable enough to be on my own. With looks and words of sincerity, I felt a blanket of comfort cover me as I accepted the gift of love she offered. At that point, I regained focus and got back my perspective and the drive in my heart.

Tammy, who was only eighteen years old at the time and fresh out of high school, made a huge sacrifice when she dropped everything, including a job, a boyfriend, and a life at Virginia Beach that she loved, to move to Radford and help me during my first semester back in school. She agreed to live in the dorms with me instead of spending more money for an apartment. The dorm rooms aren't very big, and don't allow for very much privacy. She didn't know anyone at Radford, and was acting completely upon faith and love. It was simply amazing and valiant.

Thanks to my younger sister, I was once again ready to go full steam ahead. It was great to have my drive and determination back, but we all knew the toughest road was still ahead.

Chapter 32

My Return To RU

I can remember my first day back at school as a person with a disability like it was yesterday. When I woke up that first morning, my sister told me that it had snowed during the night and that it was still snowing. I couldn't believe it. I was a little nervous because it was my first time dealing with snow. I really didn't know how my wheelchair would handle in it. It definitely added to the stress that I was already feeling about going to class that day. I dreaded facing people whom I hadn't seen since my accident. I was so concerned about my appearance and what people would think and say about me. I knew that it was going to be a shock for some of my friends and even more so for people who knew me but weren't aware that I had been in an accident.

The loss of over fifty pounds in the six months since my accident played a major factor in the way my body reacted to weather. My "Gramps" Skinner always used to say, "You need to eat more, boy, and put some meat on your bones to help keep you warm!"

Unfortunately, now it doesn't matter how much food I eat. I no longer have control of my body temperature, which is yet another joy that comes along with being a quadriplegic. We all have an autonomic nervous system that controls and regulates many things throughout our body, including our temperature. Due to the level of my injury, I don't have any control of my autonomic nervous system, therefore, it doesn't function the same way that yours would. Having no control over my body temperature makes it very difficult to maintain a comfort level in extreme temperatures. When I get cold, it is very difficult to warm up and vice versa when it is hot outside. I can get overheated easily and it is extremely difficult to cool down. I knew because it was so cold outside, it was going to be a miserable day.

I remember rolling to the end of the hallway and stopping just before I went outside. I sat and stared out the windows in the doors, dreading what was before me. My dorm was located in a central location, which made it hands down the busiest intersection on campus. The first thing I noticed as I gazed out the windows was the snow still pouring down from the sky and accumulating on the railing in front of me. To me, it was not a comfortable or beautiful thing.

Then my focus went beyond the snow. I saw students walking to and from class, going about their daily lives, and this really terrified me. The thought of having to face people that I knew before my accident became my biggest fear. I hated the way that they looked at me and always wondered what they were thinking. Because I was so active on campus before my accident, in an off-campus fraternity and as a big brother for a sorority, I knew many people. In my mind, that only made things more difficult.

That first day, and each day for weeks to come, I must have turned around and gone back to my room at least a dozen times. I would just sit at the end of the hallway staring out the windows with tears of fear rolling down my cheeks. The whole time I was sitting there, I would try to psych myself up to face the world by repeating to myself, "Come on Skinner, this is what you came here for. You can do it. Just put your hand on the little plastic joystick and push forward." Needless to say, it was much easier said than done!

Finally, I reached down put my hand on the joystick and

pushed through the door beginning my journey. I took things nice and slow, not wanting to mess up and bring any extra attention my way. I tried to focus directly in front of me, not making eye contact with anyone, because of insecurities in myself. I felt very uncomfortable and I don't think I said a word to anyone the whole way to class. I remembered what my friend from rehab, Robin Clark, told me, "You have to be comfortable with yourself before you can expect other people to be comfortable with you."

Robin Clark was like an Obi-Wan Kenobi from *Star Wars,* always coming to my mind in times of need with words of wisdom.

Entering my first class, I felt like all eyes were upon me as paranoia set in. I was still focusing in front of me, taking things easy, when I realized there was only one spot in the entire classroom where a wheelchair could fit. It was a tough turn to maneuver into the spot. Because of the snow, my wheels were wet and making a loud screeching noise with every turn. I was nervous until I noticed that sitting next to the spot was a cute blond haired girl. I suddenly felt a smile sneak on my face.

Oh yeah, that's what I'm talking about. I'm starting off right where I left off.

She took my mind off of everything I was thinking about and for the first time, I felt fairly comfortable. The feeling didn't last long.

As we made brief eye contact, I saw that she realized that I was going to be sitting next to her. Judging by her mannerisms and the look on her face, I got the impression that she was starting to feel a bit uncomfortable. At this point, I really wasn't aware that it was because of me. I thought that maybe I was just being too presumptuous. After I was finally settled in my spot and I had a free moment, I turned to her and said,

"Hello."

Getting no response I thought she probably didn't hear me and decided to try again a little louder this time. So I leaned toward her and tried again,

"Hey there, how are you?"

Judging from her response, you would have thought I was a monster from the Michael Jackson video, *Thriller*. She packed up all of her stuff and moved to the back of the room without saying a word.

Sitting there in front of that classroom, it took everything I had not to burst out in tears. At no point in my life have I ever felt so ugly and out of place. I gritted my teeth so hard I'm surprised they didn't shatter into a million pieces. This was the first real face-to-face reality check about my appearance and my disability that I encountered. I was so mad.

Even a dog says hello to you by wagging its tail when you say hi. It is just simply common courtesy, I thought.

I sat and pondered this situation. I realized that up to this point I had been around people who didn't treat me differently. I had only been at rehab centers, and around my family. Right then, at that very moment, I realized and didn't want to accept the reality of who I was and what I had become.

Leaving class that day, I held my head low and felt disgusted with myself, which only made people even more uncomfortable about my situation. I went back to my dorm room crying and called my mother. I told her to come get me, that I had made a big mistake. She told me to calm down and then encouraged me by telling me how proud she was of me for being so strong and courageous.

After experiencing this huge letdown, going out in public for the first time and to my very first class, I didn't want to leave my room. I wanted to just sit behind closed doors where no one could see me. I wanted to just feel sorry for myself for a while. Every time someone would come by and try to get me to come somewhere, I would say no and make up some sort of excuse. I didn't want to face that reality again, which made reality reluctant to face me. I absolutely hated looking into the mirror. Every time I looked in the mirror, all I could think about was the night of the accident and what decisions I could have made differently that would have changed the outcome. I frustrated myself to death thinking I could have done this, or I could have done that.

That is why you and I have to realize how important each and every decision is. We have to make each decision wisely, as if it can have a lasting impact on our life, because it can!

For several weeks I went straight to class and then straight back to my room, the whole time keeping my head down so I wouldn't have to look at anyone. I didn't even leave my room when it was time for meals. I had my sister and other close friends go and get the food for me.

One of the sorority sisters, Maureen, was an acquaintance of mine before my accident. She really surprised me by her compassion. Maureen continuously stuck by me day and night becoming one of my best friends. She would always try everything in her power to get me to go out of my room and do things. She majored in recreational therapy so she was always coming up with different things for us to do. I was consistent in my efforts to remain a hermit, quick to turn down her ideas with some sort of excuse. After several weeks of excuses and attitudes, she finally got fed up and put her foot down.

She said before she left, "That's it, Chris Skinner, I am not going to come over here anymore if you do not start coming out of this room!"

At that point, we were halfway through the semester and she was one of the only friends I had. I couldn't stand the possibility of her not coming over and me being alone. I knew that

I would miss her companionship if I didn't comply, so within a half hour after she left, I called her and told her I was willing to go out and about.

That is exactly what we did. I started getting out of my room more and more each day, exploring the campus. Going around campus was really hard for me, being on my old stomping grounds again, but this time from the perspective of a wheelchair. Seeing benches I used to sit on, fields I used to play sports in, streets I used to drive on, houses I used to party in, and people I used to hang out with knocked the wind out of me. It seemed like yesterday that I was an able-bodied person running around the campus like everyone else. I sat in astonishment as I realized how quickly one's life could change. In a split-second, with one decision, our lives can go from the way we are used to living to being turned upside down and all around. This is such a scary reality that we all need to be aware it can happen.

While I was rolling around campus, it crushed me to see the look on some people's faces when they laid eyes on me. It was as if the eye contact knocked the wind out of them as well, and I couldn't begin to explain how badly that hurt me inside. I think what hurt the most was the realization that for the rest of my life every time I go out into public, I will have to come face-to-face with individuals who have never seen someone in my situation before.

I never knew how a person was going to react. Some people acted completely normal as if they would with anyone else. Then there were the nervous types who didn't really know what to say, so they said nothing at all. I won't forget the curious types, who would, sometimes without realizing it, sit there and stare at me probably wondering, "what in the world happened to that guy," or "that poor unfortunate boy." Now I am sure that there were also several who were thinking, "what a really neat looking wheelchair that guy's in," but at that particular stage of my life, I couldn't see the positive side.

I have often heard people say that they wouldn't even begin to know what to say to someone in a wheelchair or with a disability. I would like to share with you just how simple it is. It is as simple as acting and talking the same way you would to anyone else, because the fact of the matter is, people with disabilities are exactly like everyone else. We smile like you, we frown like you, we bleed like you, and we feel sad, mad, frustrated, happy, and joyful, just like you. It always reminds me of a song in the Walt Disney version of *The Jungle Book*. The king of the monkeys sings "I wanna be like you" to the man-child because he wants to be human. We are all human, so let's treat each other that way!

One day, I happened to overhear one of my friends say, "Oh, man, I can't stand to see Skinner like that! That poor guy; he should just go home."

That was such a hurtful thing to overhear. I closed my eyes and put my head down, gritting my teeth, and felt an unbearable pain inside. As I mentioned before, several people that I thought were my friends disappointed me when I was in the hospital. For some reason, I always thought that when I came face-to-face with them it was going to be different. It was so odd to me how, in just six months, the memory of some of these people and our relationships changed so drastically. Some of my friends just weren't able to deal with the change, so they avoided me altogether. I actually had one friend who admitted that when she saw me on campus, she would purposely make a giant loop around me so that she didn't have to come face-to-face with me. Hearing this made me hysterically upset at first, then it made me furious. I realized that several of my friends were doing the exact same thing. I couldn't believe that people our age could be so childish and ignorant.

I'm not the type to brood or be angry for long. I tried to see the situation from their point of view. After some reflection, my philosophy on this matter is this. Many of my friends, who basically disappeared, did so to keep from facing the reality of this situation and its severity. I believe that if and when they came face-to-face with me, it was a truthful, harsh reminder to them that they are not invincible. They realized that they were making some of the same decisions that I made, which ultimately led to my paralysis. I believe the thought of that scared them. Instead of facing me and the reality of the situation, or better yet, changing their ways, they chose to turn their backs completely, as if they were ignoring the fact that it ever happened, and could happen to them. It was a valuable lesson, which led me to look back at myself and evaluate what type of person I was. It also made me aware of what type of person I do not want to be.

What type of person are you? I beg of you not to turn your back on any opportunity to learn valuable lessons from life. Instead, stand face-to-face with them and learn from them.

I didn't want people to feel sorry for me or think I was unfortunate. My perception of myself was completely different. I still felt like the same old Skinner (goofy, fun-loving, outgoing, good-looking, and ready to get into anything). I wouldn't have come back to school and gone all out if I felt I was poor and unfortunate. I was just doing what I knew best, being myself. That's all I expected from everyone else, to be themselves and act naturally. I guess that is exactly what they were doing. They were being themselves, and unfortunately, several of those so-called friends weren't exactly who I thought they were. This was a hard lesson to learn, especially at this hard time in my life. I constantly battled with it in my mind, asking myself endless questions.

How could they turn their backs on me?

Why do they think I am different now?

Doesn't it bother them at all that we aren't talking anymore?

Did they really forget about me already?

Were we ever friends in the first place?

Is this the way I would act in their shoes?

I just wanted to say "Hey guys, it's me Skin-dog." Unfortunately, I know it wouldn't have done any good. Those particular individuals knew exactly who I was. I just didn't know who they were until my traumatic experience. It is amazing to me how I went through life, especially college, and never knew who my real friends were until tragedy struck!

Do you know who your real friends are? I encourage you to take time and evaluate whom you spend your time with. Do they build you up and encourage you to become a better person? Would they be there for you if tragedy struck?

My pity party didn't last long. Getting upset because of other people got old pretty fast. It didn't make any sense to let something or someone that I had absolutely no control over affect how I thought or felt. The fact of the matter is we can't control the way other people act. We can only control our perspectives, our actions, and ourselves. At that point, when I was finally able to accept the fact that things were going to be different, I started to move on and enjoy what blessings life still had in store for me. I reminded myself daily of Robin's attitude and my vow not to focus on the things that I didn't have, but instead to focus on the things that I do have.

No matter who you are in this world or what you may be dealing with, these particular experiences I have shared with you thus far have got be a wake-up call of some sort. My continuous reality check was thinking about seeing that young boy paralyzed from the neck down in rehab. Thinking about that horrifying picture always helped to humble me. Think of all the blessings that you have in your life and be thankful for them. Different doesn't necessarily mean something bad. Some change is for the better! My physical appearance doesn't necessarily show it as far as society goes, but the insight and wisdom I have developed internally is priceless.

My grandfather, Henry Wells, once told me that he believed that all people are good people deep down inside. Most people, he would say, feel great joy and pleasure in doing things to help others. As far as my experiences go as a person with a disability, he was right. There were many people who surprised me with their level of commitment and compassion by stepping up and becoming better friends. There were several people who I wasn't necessarily close to at all before my accident, who gave their time to help me in any way. Before the accident, they were just acquaintances, or people I would just smile at and say hello. At times, when these individuals would help me with things, I would feel ashamed of myself because of the way I acted toward them before my accident. They didn't owe me anything; in fact, I probably owed most of them an apology of some sort. These were some of the people my grandfather was talking about.

Still others were complete strangers who would go out of their way to try and help. If I were rolling up to a doorway, students on campus would go out of their way, running ahead of me to help open the door. Just little things, like a smile here and a hello there, made all the difference in the world. I encourage everyone each day to go out of his or her way and try to do something nice for someone else. You never know, and would probably be surprised, how much of an impact you can have on someone's life and vice versa. I believe what you give comes back to you twofold. The simple act of encouraging others lifts our own spirits as well.

I began to feel more and more comfortable on campus going to and from class and hanging out in the dining halls as the semester went on. So much so that I started thinking about what was going on off-campus, which was not a good thing. The more confident I became, the more I thought about the life I used to live and things I used to do. It started to consume my thoughts. I thought about my fraternity, other fraternities, and the bars. I would daydream about the socializing, the girls, the alcohol, and the drugs. That was the lifestyle that I was good at, and where I was able to make up the rules as I went along. Irrationally, I thought this was the only lifestyle where I'd be able to fit in and be accepted. These thoughts were like cancer. Once I started thinking about them again, they poured in, spreading through my mind and consuming my every thought. I held to these cancerous thoughts so desperately that I began to crave them. That is the way that life is. We allow our minds to be consumed by temptation and desires. The next step then could very well be that our thoughts lead to actions.

That is exactly what happened to me all over again. I began sliding right back into the situation I was involved in before my accident, where I lost touch with reality and eventually life as I knew it. I was lonely and felt like there were holes in my heart that needed to be filled. Unfortunately, the only way at this point in my life that I knew how to fill those holes was to fall victim to temptation, and go out intentionally to alter my state of consciousness with alcohol and drugs. Alcohol and drugs are just a temporary fix. They lead to nothing good in life. All of the alcohol, all of the drugs, and all of the socializing mixed with it is what I call temporary fun. Every situation involving drugs or alcohol that I have either been involved in or heard about has always resulted in some sort of negative consequences. Just think about this. When people go out and get drunk, at that time it seems like they are having so much fun. Later on that night when they are hugging the toilet bowl and begging for mercy, it is not so much fun anymore. If and when they finally fall asleep, they awaken to a world full of headaches. This is just a small example of what the choice of temporary fun can bring to your life.

The part that tears me up inside is that even knowing from first-hand experience that this particular attitude and life-style only brought temporary happiness to my life, I continued my pursuit of it. It's ridiculous that I came face-to-face with death all because of this temporary fun, and then still pursued it when I was given a second chance. Is that fair?

My Aunt Janice was killed in an automobile accident by a seventeen-year-old drunk driver. She wasn't given a second chance. There are thousands of other individuals who chose temporary fun and received no second chance. I not only wasn't learning from others, I wasn't learning from my own mistakes. What about you? Are you learning from other people's mistakes? Equally important, are you learning from your own mistakes? I often questioned myself, *how can you be so weak and stupid? How can you go back to the same hopelessness that almost took your life, and caused you, your family, and your friends so much pain? How? Why?"*

Behind closed doors I called these questions aloud. Out of doors, I began expressing my interest in going out to everyone I came in contact with. Most of the people I knew were involved in, at least occasionally, some sort of party life. My goal was for someone to invite me out so it didn't seem like I was initiating the plan. I tried my hardest to make it sound like I was just talking about it, and not really wanting to do it. There was much more to it than that. I had ulterior motives that no one knew about. I was being sneaky, and intended to get back on the scene and test my limits.

Someone eventually took the bait and asked me to come out to a fraternity party with them. Without hesitation, because that was exactly what I wanted to happen, I accepted the invitation. I went out to the fraternity party and then to bars with some friends searching for happiness in an environment that was full of hopelessness. It is impossible to find happiness in these situations.

As we journey through our lives, we need to remember that. Many times we get caught up in the moment, thinking that we are experiencing true joy as opposed to temporary happiness or temporary fun. There is a major difference between the two. Happiness is temporary and driven by our emotions. It is like opening a present on Christmas day and being so thrilled with your new toy, only to throw it away or lose track of it in a matter of months. How many of you have experienced this?

True joy on the other hand is eternal. It doesn't depend on an emotion and can be experienced even in the worst of situations. It comes from the heart and not from feelings. It comes from positive knowledge and experiences that can't be erased or forgotten. Have you experienced true joy?

At first, I had a lot of fun because I was back in the spotlight. People at the bar that I hadn't seen or heard from in months were suddenly my best friends again, offering me beer, buying me shots, and talking about old times again as if nothing ever happened. It felt great. The more intoxicated we got, the better things seemed and the more comfortable everyone felt being around me. While drinking and partying, I was being the Chris Skinner that everyone knew, accepted, and still wanted to be with. People would give me their telephone numbers telling me to call them if I ever needed anything. At the same time, they would promise to stop by and hang out sometime.

People so often live by the moment not thinking about the consequences that could come out of their decisions that are being made. I know I am guilty! We are always banking on the fact that the sun is going to set tonight and rise again tomorrow morning. I know that is exactly what I was thinking on June 10, 2000, and here I was again banking on the same ignorant concept. I'm telling you from experience it doesn't work that way, especially when you choose the lifestyle of temporary fun. The majority of the time things just aren't what they seem, and individuals will find themselves looking back wondering what in the world happened as soon as reality sets in.

When reality set in and all the alcohol wore off, I was given excuses when I called for help. Nine times out of ten, no one would stop by the room to see me. When we were drunk together, the temporary fun was great. When we were sober, however, reality set in all over again. It was so ironic that every time they laid eyes on me sober they didn't know how to act. Here again, we see how people were frightened by my situation because of the reality check it gave them. The constant reminder of how fragile the human body is, and how dangerous each and every decision we make can be, is often too much to handle. Instead of facing this truth, many people choose to turn their head from it and pretend it didn't and couldn't happen to them. It is just like the saying, "out of sight, out of mind." If we don't have to see something or deal with it directly, then it doesn't affect us. I challenge you not to be this close-minded in your life.

For a couple of months, I continued this pattern of going out, getting intoxicated, feeling accepted, and then waking up the next morning and feeling rejected. Once again, I had fallen to temptation and lies. I was so afraid of losing approval from the people I used to hang around that I couldn't quite get myself together. I started to feel miserable and hopeless once again, only this time I knew that what I was doing was completely ignorant. I wanted so badly to express to everyone how dangerous alcohol and drugs can be. I wanted to be a good influence and change people's perspectives and attitude toward social life in general. The only problem was that I was having a hard time with changing myself.

I was being a complete hypocrite. I had to come to the realization that I wasn't the same Chris Skinner that I used to be. I was a changed man on the inside, through my thoughts and ideas, and now I had to be a changed man on the outside through my actions. We all know it is easier to talk the talk than to walk the walk. In other words, I knew what I wanted to do and was supposed to do, but I just couldn't put it into action.

I began to develop a deep passion to share my experiences and strive to help others. It started with my opportunities to talk with my drunken friends while I was at the bars with them. My heart would leap out at the chance to share with anyone about what happened to me.

Chapter 33

My Ultimate Learning Experience

Before my accident during my freshman year, I had gotten into some trouble in my dorm room because of alcohol and drugs. As part of my disciplinary consequences, I had to contact a woman, Ms. McGuire, who worked in New Student Programs at Radford University and set up times during which I would share with the incoming freshmen my experience with alcohol and drugs and how it affected me negatively. Of course, I never went through with it, because I was suspended from school before I ever had the chance to talk with them. Remembering this, I contacted the same woman and asked her if she would allow me to share my experience with the freshmen. She agreed, but asked to review what I was planning to share with them. I told her that would be awesome, but I hadn't yet put my presentation together. I then told her that I would put one together and call her for a meeting.

In one sitting, I put together a PowerPoint presentation with pictures displaying my life before partying, during partying, and the results after partying. While I was sitting at the computer that day, putting my life on PowerPoint, I envisioned all the good that could come from my situation and the story of my life. After several hours of work, when I was finally finished, I sat back and smiled at what I was able to accomplish. I remember sitting there, thinking to myself, *Man, this journey sure has been the **ultimate of experiences.***

The next week I called Ms. McGuire and presented, for the first time, "The Ultimate Learning Experience!" She seemed very impressed with what I had done and asked me how many times I thought I would be able to make this presentation. With a big smile on my face, I told her as many times as possible!

Just a few weeks later I put my passion into practice as I shared "The Ultimate Learning Experience" with a freshman orientation class at Radford University, called University 100. I was so incredibly excited to be able to share my experience with a group of students with the thought of possibly saving lives. I remember the first group of students I spoke with just like it was yesterday. It was the second week of school and there were about one hundred incoming freshmen sitting restlessly in a little auditorium. I arrived early and sat in my wheelchair watching the interactions between the students, and remembering what it was like being in their shoes. I started thinking if they were anything like me, they were probably gearing themselves up to hear some cheesy speech about alcohol during which they would glance at their watch every five minutes, eagerly waiting for the speaker to shut up so that they could go about their day. I didn't want them to look at me as another authority figure in their life, pointing the finger and saying, "don't do this or that." I didn't want to give the same lecture they had most likely heard over and over again since the third grade on the dangers of alcohol and drugs. I remembered those types of lectures and the effect they had on me. You can tell that they obviously didn't affect me enough.

With that in mind as the time came closer for me to speak, my heart became burdened. I needed to reach each and every one of the students in some way. My goal was to be honest, sincere, compassionate, and vulnerable in a funny, yet serious, manner in order to captivate their attention.

During the 2001 spring semester at Radford University, I felt my passion increase each and every time I presented my experience. For the first time, I felt as if I knew what I was called to do with the rest of my life. I was on fire and so excited about my calling that I could hardly sleep. When I finally slept, I dreamt of speaking to large crowds and reaching out to millions of people all over the world.

You might think that is where the story ends, but remember I still was battling the concept of talking the talk and walking the walk. Yes, I was speaking to hundreds of freshmen and probably making a significant impact on some of their lives, but the fact of the matter was, I was still a hypocrite. I was telling the students how dangerous alcohol and drugs are and to stay away from them, yet at the same time, I was still involved with them myself. I always felt a small sense of pride after my speeches when students would come up to me and tell me how much of an inspiration I was to them, how they were going to start thinking about their decisions, and how they were going to make a point to try and stay away from alcohol and drugs.

Although I am certain I probably could have continued to get away with this behavior and still impact lives, the feeling of not being honest with them and most importantly, with myself started to weigh upon my heart. We may be able to get away with some lie without anyone ever knowing, but in the long run, it will affect us because we know. Sooner or later, you will feel the consequences. Either your conscience will bring you down or someone will eventually catch you in your dishonesty. Then all of your deception will come crashing down right before your very eyes. Depending on how grave the error, possibly all your dreams and aspirations could be affected as well.

Deep down inside of me I really meant every word that I said at every speech, and sincerely wanted others to realize how precious life is. I didn't want anyone to have to experience what I had gone through, or worse. I knew that there had to be a change in my life or the words from my experience and the mission to save lives would be compromised.

At this point I started realizing what was important and what wasn't. I knew that being honest and speaking from my heart would make me happy and allow my presentation to be much more powerful. I believe people have the ability to see intuitively through you, so to speak. Have you ever talked to someone and felt that they were not being sincere with you? I did not want people to look at me and feel like I was insincere. I started searching for individuals who exemplified sincerity and truth. I wanted more than anything for people to be able to look at my actions and want to follow me. In essence, I wanted to be a good leader.

One of my nursing aides, Emilee, fit the description of sincerity and truth to the tenth degree. I started asking her questions about her life and her beliefs. She made me realize a few things, including how much I had forgotten since my childhood. She told me she was a Christian, and that she loved God and her experiences with her church community more than anything in this world. When I heard her speak of these things with such passion and joy, it made me realize that I used to be part of things like that and I had fun with them. Then one day I asked her if I could go to church with her and she answered with a great big smile.

"Of course you can, that would be great!"

When I first started attending church with Emilee, I was just observing the whole scene. You might say I was "just testing the waters." As I met other people in the church community, I can't explain to you how loved and accepted I felt. Everyone seemed so positive and upbeat. The other students with whom I began developing friendships were surprisingly focused on their goals and didn't seem to worry about where the parties were or what was going on in the bars. They had a peace about them that allowed their actions to glow, and I wanted that same peace and glow. I was completely shocked when several of these individuals asked for my telephone number and then within days actually called me and came by to visit. It was awesome!

I mentioned earlier that when I gave my speeches, I always felt a small sense of guilt because of my actions outside of the presentations. I didn't go out and get drunk, but the fact that someone might see me with a drink in my hand and assume the worst worried me. I knew that I wanted to completely do away with the hypocritical feelings I felt. It just so happened that after sharing this with my friends who were Christians and having them pray for me, I had an experience that I needed in order to completely turn my life in the right direction.

While I was trying to re-establish my roots with church and God, I got an opportunity to speak at a local high school on Friday, September 27, 2001. I was extremely excited that I was able to share my experience with high school students. This was my first big step in pursuing my dream of being a public speaker because it was my first speaking engagement outside of Radford University.

When I arrived at the high school, I felt my nerves kicking in, as usual. My stomach was full of butterflies. I was led to the library where I was going to deliver my presentation to a group of eleventh graders. I went through my presentation as I always did, with confidence and passion. When I finally came to the end of my presentation, I offered to answer any questions concerning my life and or the presentation. As the students began firing away, complimenting me and asking questions concerning my accident, I began to feel a sense of pride because of the impact I felt like I was making and it made me happy.

This feeling of pride and happiness came to a complete halt as I was convicted once and for all. For the rest of my life, I will never forget the young lady or question that she asked. Oddly enough, she was the only student who actually stood up when she asked her question. Standing boldly she asked, "Didn't I see you last week at a fraternity party drinking alcohol?"

At that moment, I felt as if someone was cutting out my heart with a spoon. I knew the entire message that I had just delivered would be completely discredited in the eyes of these eleventh graders. They all sat staring deep into my soul, awaiting my answer. For a split second, I actually thought about lying. I started to tell the students, "No that wasn't me, it must have been someone else," when my conscience took over and I was guided to speak the truth. I suddenly remembered how I longed for sincerity and truth and even asked people to pray for it in my life. At that moment, even though I felt that being honest would discredit my message, I replied,

"Yes, I was at a fraternity party last week drinking."

There was a deafening silence in the room. No other students asked questions that day. When I was leaving the school parking lot, my eyes filled with tears, my heart felt like it stopped beating, and I lowered my head in disgrace. I was disgusted with my past actions and myself. Right then and there, I vowed to make a change in my life, to sacrifice my old lifestyle and my old habits, and to better my future and the future of others.

The beauty of life is that no matter who you are or what you have done throughout your life, you can change for the better. You can make the conscious decision at any time to change directions in your life and get on the right path. We have to realize that yesterday doesn't matter today! There is nothing that we can do about what has happened to us, or by us, in the past. Please don't misunderstand; I am not saying that we can't change some things about our past, because we can. We can always find the individuals we have hurt, apologize, and ask for their forgiveness. We can forgive the individuals who have hurt us.

What I am strongly implying is that the only real control we have is the ability to make decisions in the here and now (the present). The ability to want to change your direction is the easy part; the hard part is actually putting your desire to change into action. There are many of us who think we can handle things all by ourselves, but I'm telling you friends, we can't. I am encouraging you to seek help and guidance from others.

Chapter 34

Searching For Truth

Now I wanted more than anything to change my decision-making process and my actions, but I wasn't sure how to do it. Immediately after I spoke at the high school, I left Radford. I went home to visit my parents in Smithfield, VA and attend a wedding in which I was asked to read scripture. I spent the entire five-hour drive home searching within myself for answers. I wasn't saying a word, but inside I was screaming out loud for help. About halfway home, I realized that I wasn't just talking to myself, I was praying to God. My whole life I thought that in order to pray you had to sit down with your hands folded together and start off by saying, "Dear God," or "Heavenly Father," but I was so wrong. I realized that day that any type of communication between you and God is a prayer. I was praying! I was asking God for help. I was asking Him to give me a sign or some sort of guidance.

On Saturday, September 29, 2001, I went to my friends' wedding and read scripture during the ceremony. When it was time to go to the reception, I started to get nervous, because this was the first wedding that I had been to since the night of my accident. The whole time I sat at the wedding and the reception, I experienced flashbacks from the night that changed my life forever. The reception I attended was relatively similar to the one on June 10, 2000. It was a beautiful night, with plenty of opportunities for someone to find temptation and make bad decisions with negative consequences. I want to point out that if you look around you can always find opportunities that involve temptation and making bad decisions. Always! There was a DJ playing music, there were plenty of single girls and guys, and to top things off, there was an open bar stocked with your favorite alcoholic drinks. All the ingredients you need to have temporary fun.

I sat at a table that night with some friends from college, scanning the scene and absorbing the atmosphere. I watched as people drank beer after beer, and mixed drink after mixed drink. I started asking questions in my mind concerning these individuals.

I wonder how many beers that person has had?

How many of these individuals will be hugging the toilet tonight?

How many are going to drive under the influence of alcohol tonight?

Which one will be the next casualty?

It was amazing to me how my perspective on situations like this had changed in just one afternoon and because of the words of one eleventh-grade girl. I was deep in thought when I finally realized that I was taking sips of a beer that one of my peers was holding for me to drink. I felt my heart burn with remorse and when offered another sip of the beer, I shook my head no and said that I had enough. Once again, because I chose not to participate in the temporary fun, this individual shrugged her shoulders and walked away from me. At this point, I could care less. I suddenly started to see life more clearly.

I suddenly felt as if someone was watching me. I didn't feel threatened by it, just a full awareness that my actions and facial expressions were being observed. When I turned my head and looked around, I saw that it was the pastor who performed the marriage ceremony for my two friends. When our eyes met, he smiled and nodded his head in a friendly way as if to say hello. After returning the nod and the smile, I felt drawn to him. All at once, I was filled with questions I wanted to ask this man, who happened to be a complete stranger. Without wasting another second, I put my hand down on that little plastic joystick that controlled my wheelchair and went straight to him, without glancing in any other direction. I was in the zone!

When I got over to him I said, "Excuse me sir, can I talk to you about something?"

Without even a slight hesitation, he replied, "Absolutely, Chris, what's on your mind?"

At first I paused because I wasn't sure how he knew my name, but then I realized that my name was on the program for the wedding. Then he said that my friends who were just married had told him a lot about me. Without wasting any time, I told him everything that had happened to me from birth until the very present, including the incident that had convicted my heart the day before.

I had never really let so much honesty and truth come out of my mouth, let alone to someone who was a complete stranger before that night, but he was such a great listener. I just felt so comfortable and knew that this man genuinely cared about what I was saying. We must have talked that night for over an hour. It was an awesome conversation. He advised me to listen to my heart and continue to communicate with God. I remember his words.

"It seems to me that you are searching and seeking the truth, but just can't seem to put your finger on it. I encourage you to keep praying to God and asking Him to show you what you need to be shown. I know that He will answer your prayers."

I left the reception that night feeling a sense of peace. Lying in bed that night, I was unable to sleep. All I could think about was what I truly wanted for my life, and how I wanted people to be able to trust every word I spoke. In essence, I wanted my yes to mean yes and my no to mean no.

Do you know someone whose words you can trust to be true and whose promises you can trust to be kept? I believe we should all strive to be men and women of irreproachable integrity. I lay in bed thinking about the pastor's words of advice, when I decided to do exactly what he advised me to do. Speaking out loud, with my eyes open, I again expressed my emotions and frustrations to God. In desperation, I then asked Him to show me how to be the man I truly wanted to be.

The next morning, September 30, 2001, my mother got me out of bed and motivated me to go to church, despite feelings of frustration and fatigue. Still battling thoughts in my mind of guilt and shame, I filed into the church smiling at people and shaking their hands. When church started, I didn't really pay attention to anything. I immediately started a conversation with God in my mind. I was going back and forth with my thoughts when a statement that the pastor made grabbed my attention.

"We need to make our actions speak louder than words!"

When I heard this, I instantly tuned in to what he was saying. Sitting in the sanctuary that day listening to the sermon, I felt as if the whole message was directed strictly to me. It almost felt as if I was the only person in the church and the pastor was talking one-on-one with me. Have any of you ever felt like this at church or in a large group? Like someone was speaking and it felt like they had been listening to your thoughts and said exactly what you needed to hear. That is how I felt as I hung on his every word. Then I started to feel my heart beat faster, my blood pressure rise, and the hair on the back of my neck stand up! I felt a change going on inside of me. I started to see before my very own eyes and feel within my heart the answer to my prayers. The pastor ended the sermon with a parable. It was a story that would forever change my life.

The parable went like this. There was a man who always went to a certain restaurant every day for lunch, because of the great feeling he had while he was there. He always noticed that there was an enchanting, indescribable fragrance in the air of this particular restaurant during the lunch hour. After months of going there to eat, he finally decided to ask one of the waitresses about the fragrance. The man called the waitress over and asked, "How do you guys do it? How do you make it smell so good in here every day during the lunch hour?"

The waitress answered with a grin on her face, "Oh, sir. It's not us that make it smell so wonderful in here. You see there is a perfume factory down the block and every day when the workers get off for lunch, they walk by our restaurant and the fragrance from their clothes lingers in here making it smell wonderful!"

The pastor paused for a second and then looked right at me as he said, "That, my friends, is what we are supposed to be like as people, and most importantly as Christians! We should be able to walk into a room or by a room and have people notice something amazing and desirable about us. They should be able to sense and feel the presence of sincerity and truth, which ultimately my friends, comes from a relationship with the Lord Jesus Christ! We must let our actions speak louder than words!"

Immediately, I started thinking about my physical therapist at Woodrow Wilson, Suzie, and my nurse at school, Emilee, who were two individuals that exemplified sincerity and truth. I also knew that these two amazing individuals were Christians who lived their lives as a daily testimony for God by allowing their actions to speak louder than words. At that moment, after twenty-one years of life, I finally realized that I couldn't go on with life without a personal relationship with Jesus Christ.

If I could have gotten out of my wheelchair that day, I would have lain flat on the floor, face down, with my arms stretched out wide and begged for forgiveness. Instead, I got into the most submissive position that I possibly could by laying my head down and dangling my arms down to my side and cried out to God.

As tears rolled down my face I spoke aloud, "Please God come into my heart and guide my life in the direction that you want it to go in! I am lost without you! "

On this day, September 30, 2001, I finally made the decision to give up the use of alcohol and drugs in my life once and for all. I felt absolutely great about my decisions and myself.

Chapter 35

Walk The Walk

When I returned to school, I felt supercharged and ready for anything. As soon as I rolled in the door, my roommate Josh instantly said to me, "Man you look great! I mean you seem so happy. What in the world happened to you this past weekend?"

I smiled as I started to think about the sermon, and about letting my actions speak louder than words.

It is working already! I thought to myself. I hadn't even said a word to him and he already noticed a difference in my life.

Josh knew me so well, now more than ever. This would be our last semester together. As I looked at my friend, I remembered all the good times we had together and how much we'd grown through the years.

Josh and I had been roommates during our freshman year in 1997–98. He asked me to allow him to be my roommate again this particular semester, for old times' sake. Josh had been living off-campus for the past three years and only had this semester left before he graduated. I always considered Josh to be a brother. I was completely honored when my friend insisted on living with me.

"We started our college careers together and I want to end my time at Radford with you. It's only fitting."

I told him how hard it would be for him. I had no privacy and neither would he. I had nurses coming at all times of the day and night to help me. They would disturb his rest and his ability to study. I was concerned about his ability to make it through his final semester successfully with all the interruptions. None of my objections deterred him.

"Come on Skinner," he said. "It will be great. You and I having our deep discussions on matters of great importance… like girls. Maybe we'll be able to figure them out before we graduate."

"I don't know, Josh. It sounds great, but I think you are getting into more than you realize. I really can't do anything for myself and I need help constantly."

"I'll help you. I can learn to do whatever you need." Josh replied.

"I don't know…it can get pretty intense." I said.

"Look, Skinner. You mean a lot to me. I would do anything in the world for you and I mean that. Anything. Nothing is too much to ask."

"Well, it would be great watching all the sports on TV with you. Josh, I can't go out as much as I used to. I stay in my room a lot more than I used to," I told him.

"Hey, Skinner. You know me, man. I don't care about that. I just want this last semester to be my gift to you. We'll do it together…and it will be fun."

And that's how we arranged it. It was that simple. Josh took it all in stride. He arranged his schedule to help me. We ate lunch and dinner together. We chilled in the evenings, doing reading assignments or watching TV.

We had plenty of lengthy discussions and most of them were about girls, sports and religion. Interesting combination I know, but that was what we were interested in. Josh was Jewish by birth, but didn't practice any religion. He took more of a scientific approach in the way that he looked at the world. So it didn't surprise me that he noticed immediately that there was a change in me.

After I explained to him that I became a Christian and decided not to drink or do drugs anymore, he had a surprising response for me.

"That's great, Skinner! I am really happy for you. But what about alumni weekend?"

I remember stopping dead in my tracks. I wasn't surprised that he was excited for me, since we always wanted the best for one another. I had totally forgotten that a bunch of my alumni fraternity brothers were coming into town and were expecting me to go out with them. That was what we typically did when there was an alumni weekend. We would always plan to get together, go out on town, and get drunk. At first I panicked, because I had already told several of the alumni guys that I was going to be participating in the weekend. In fact, I had arranged for some of them to come by my dorm room when they arrived to help get me to the parties. For a second, I thought about just telling everyone that I wasn't feeling well so that I didn't have to go at all. Then it hit me straight in the face. This would be my first test of whether or not I was going to let my actions speak louder than words.

I said to my roommate boldly, "I know it is alumni weekend and I still plan on going out with the guys I just don't intend to drink or do drugs. I will show them by my actions how serious I am about the dangers of alcohol and drugs!"

He gave me a look of disbelief and said, "Okay, well good luck man!"

The weekend came, and with it came the alumni. Right from the start, I knew things were going to be difficult. The first couple of guys that I saw immediately wanted to go to the bars and get drinks. Within a matter of minutes, I was asked the question which I had prepared myself for all week.

"What would you like to drink Skinner?" one of the guys asked.

"I don't drink anymore," I responded.

With a giggle, another individual asked, "since when?"

I started to get a little bit nervous and anxious until I remembered my experience with the 11th grade girl, and my commitment to live fully for God, staying away from temporary fun like this.

"Since last weekend," I answered firmly.

There were a couple more giggles and comments of disbelief, but I stood my ground and continued to stand up for what I believed in. It is hard to stand up for what you believe is right, especially when it could mean the possibility of hindering relationships. We have to remember that our real friends will love and stand by us no matter what. In fact, there were some guys who encouraged me and were happy for me. Some guys even replied, "That's great Skinner! I wish I could do that!"

To these guys, I was able to reply in a constructive manner.

"You can do it, if you really want to. It is just a matter of setting your cup down!"

I don't know if anyone quit drinking or not, but it was still an awesome feeling to see the looks on their faces and to be able to make them think differently about their actions. It is a great feeling to know that through your actions you have the potential to change people's perspectives and lives. The rest of the night and the weekend pretty much went the same way with people putting alcohol in front of my face and me turning it down. It seemed like everywhere I went, people were just going straight for the temporary fun. In the end, I was able to stand my ground and not give in to peer pressure. I'm telling you it was, and is, one of the best sensations in the world to conquer temptation and continue life on the right track, focusing on your goals! I highly recommend it.

After surviving that weekend, I was supercharged and totally focused on my goals. I went to my classes determined and fired up to succeed! I got involved with positive extracurricular activities such as Campus Crusades for Christ, study groups, and outdoor recreation activities. I even joined an academic fraternity that focuses on leadership called Omicron Delta Kappa. I was enjoying life and flying high, full speed ahead toward my goals. Although it wasn't easy by any means, I constantly reminded myself to take things one day at a time. As I mentioned before, we can't turn back time and we certainly can't fast-forward time, so we have to live in the "now," making our decisions wisely, from the time we wake until we go to sleep at night.

With this new perspective, I just felt like a better person all around. When I came back to school, I had a cumulative GPA of a 1.142. After putting my heart, mind, and soul into my schoolwork, I finished my last 72 credit hours with a GPA of around a 3.75. I never dreamed of making the Dean's List, but I finished my last three semesters with straight A's. I accomplished this by staying away from temporary fun, getting to know my teachers, completing all of my assignments, and attending all of my classes. I believe if you adhere to these four simple applications you will be successful with your academics.

It is so amazing to me when I think about the potential we all have to be successful. Think about it for a minute. I was exactly the same kid coming back to school, except this time, I had less going for me. Right? Wrong. Often, society focuses on the external or materialistic things rather than focusing on the most important thing, our internal self. It is true that I had lost all of my physical capabilities. Did that stop me? The fact of the matter is that we are blessed with some of the most important virtues in life: determination, willpower, ambition, desire, patience, and most importantly perseverance! Using these virtues in our everyday life enables us to accomplish our goals!

Words cannot express how great I felt on the day of my college graduation! As I sat in my cap and gown awaiting my name to be called, I felt tears forming in my eyes. I contemplated all that my family and I had been through to get to this point. I frequently looked at my entire family and gave thanks to God for such loving support. I remembered all too well the time I spent lying in a hospital bed, only capable of blinking my eyes. I thought of all the hard work and determination that brought me to this moment…and I remembered the love.

The time came for everyone in my row to stand up and go receive the diploma that we all had worked so hard for. As everyone started to stand around me I looked down at my black wheelchair and smiled proudly. At that given moment, it didn't matter to me whether I was lying down, sitting down, or turned upside down. I was fired up with excitement. I was on my way up to the front to shake hands with the President of Radford University, Dr. Covington, and receive my diploma.

The closer I got to the front the more emotional I became, as my heart started beating faster, my blood pressure raised, and I started getting giant butterflies in my stomach. When I heard my name called I felt tears form in my eyes. They remained as I rolled across the stage. I wanted to really soak up this moment, so I consciously blocked out everyone in the auditorium and focused on the Presidents' handshake and the diploma that he slid through my curled up fingers. When I thought everything was said and done, I began to turn around.

Dr. Covington stopped me and said, "I have something for you." He reached inside his royal looking robe, which had all sorts of colorful tassels and medals hanging off it, and pulled out a personalized letter written specifically for me. I felt extremely honored. Especially when he said, "I have been following your progress and I am very proud of what you have accomplished!"

"Thank you, sir," I said, then turned around and rolled off of the stage elated.

I rolled back to my row and had a classmate open the letter for me. As I read the encouraging words from President Covington, I thanked God for guiding me with His strength, and using me as a positive instrument. At the same time, I couldn't stop thinking about my next goal and how I would obtain it. I believe in life we should set goals continuously, always pressing forward, putting one foot in front of the other. I am not saying your goal always has to be life changing or profound. I am simply trying to encourage you to always lean forward and reach out for what you want, because with a little bit of patience and determination, someday you'll grab it.

Remember back when I woke up in the hospital bed paralyzed from the shoulders down wishing I would just die? That was when I didn't think I had anything else to offer the world. In reality I did have something to offer, and still do. I firmly believe that everyone has something to offer this world. No matter how down you feel, don't ever give up!

All of the, "you can't do that," and the "you're not able," meant absolutely nothing. I had accomplished my goal—period, end of chapter, and close the book! No one can ever take your accomplishments away from you. They are yours to keep, forever, in your heart! I will always cherish this milestone in my life. When you are striving to achieve your goals, always take one day at a time. When adversity comes, remember there is always a bright shining light at the end of the tunnel!

Chapter 36

Four Keys To Success

You have just about come to the end of the story of how I became who I am today. Like I mentioned in the introduction, I now have a disability that can be seen by the naked eye. It is my hope that you can understand now why I believe I had a different disability all along, and how you too might have a disability. The word disability is a label that society places on individuals who are different or who face disadvantages. In fact, the Merriam-Webster dictionary uses this definition for disability: a disqualification, restriction, or disadvantage. I am extremely confident in saying that the majority of us in some way shape or form fit into one of these three categories.

That makes all of us persons with disabilities. I know that might not sit well with some of you, and rightly so. Nobody likes to think that they are disqualified, restricted, or disadvantaged, but the fact of the matter is that we are. For the most part, we do this to ourselves, with the decisions we make throughout our lives. You read all about my physical disability, and also my disability to learn from others, make decisions wisely, and think about consequences. This ultimately led me to disqualification, restriction, and disadvantage. You saw that these disabled choices occurred before and after my car accident. My hope and prayer for everyone who reads this book is that you walk away with a new perspective on life that enables you to go out and be the productive citizen in life that you are fully capable of being.

To help you achieve this I would like to share with you my four personal keys to success. These four keys are very simple and practical, but I am positive that if you follow them as a guideline for your life, you will be successful. First, however, I will share with you my definition of success, because it may be different from yours. I am not talking about how much money you make, what your status in life is, or what kind of car you drive. My definition of being successful is simply living a healthy and happy life.

I don't believe that any person on this planet is better than another. I believe that as long as you are doing the best that you possibly can with whatever you are doing, and you feel happy with your situation, then you are a successful individual.

Key #1—Learn from others.

Let me start off by asking a question. How many of you have heard of someone or known someone who has been either injured, killed, or just had something negative happen in their lives because of alcohol and drugs?

I believe that every single one of you has encountered these negative effects. I say this because we all have seen reports on TV, in the newspaper, in our community, or in our own family. If, for some reason, you are still shaking your head no and you have read my book all the way to this point, then you can go ahead and start shaking your head yes. We know that these negative incidents are real, and are all around us, yet for some strange reason, we (as a society) continue to allow the problems to continue. I often asked myself, why? Why would anyone do something that they know for certain can bring disaster into his or her life? Please take a moment and ask yourself that question. After you have thought about it, I am sure that you would agree with my conclusion that it doesn't make any sense at all!

When I think about this concept and my life, I feel a tremendous amount of pain in my heart. You see, I had experienced firsthand the awful consequences that alcohol and drugs can bring to a family, a long time before my accident. When I was six months old, my Aunt Janice was killed in an alcohol related accident. She was eighteen years old and had a baby boy named Micah who was five months old. She was driving home from a wedding reception, completely sober and innocent of any wrongdoing, when tragedy struck. Another young woman, just seventeen, was driving intoxicated and hit my aunt's vehicle head on as they came over a bridge. My aunt's car was knocked off the bridge and it rolled down the hill into a creek. She died that night. A piece of glass from the windshield went directly into her head, killing her instantly. My cousin Micah was raised by my grandparents, and still mourns the loss of his mother to this day.

Throughout my whole life, I knew about this accident and saw the pain it caused my family. I remember visiting her gravesite and watching my cousin get on his hands and knees, ripping grass out of the ground around the tombstone and crying out for answers. I remember these moments touched me so much. I would cry with him the whole time we were there, and on the ride home afterwards.

The main reason I share this with you is to emphasize the importance of learning from others. Sometimes I feel ashamed that I could be so stupid—to drink and drive when the destruction of alcohol was in front me my entire life. This is why it is so important in our lives to be aware of what happens around us. If we can somehow consciously pay attention to the things that are happening around us, we can take what we learn from those situations and apply them to our lives.

It is my hope that my story has had a profound impact on all of you. It is my hope that every person who reads this story will decide to make the right decisions concerning alcohol and drugs. Personally, I would love for everyone to be responsible and stay away from negative opportunities altogether. I believe drugs and alcohol are like cancer with the potential to creep through your body and eventually destroy your life. My hope for you is that you will take this learning experience as your own and avoid the pain of experiencing it for yourself. I want you to learn from my mistakes and from those of others you will encounter in your life. The reality of the situation is that some of you will still decide to participate in temporary fun by involving yourself with alcohol and drugs. I know this and so do you. I challenge you to prove me wrong!

Key #2—Make your decisions wisely.

Every single day when you wake up and get out of bed, you are faced with thousands of decisions. Isn't that wild to think about? We can't even begin to count the number of decisions that we have made throughout our lifetime. If you sit and think about the decisions that you have made in the past, I am certain that you will be able to break down and figure out why you are where you are today. Some of you have done this before. It can be very painful. Keep in mind what I said in the introduction about sitting still and being honest with ourselves. These types of challenges can help us grow as individuals. I think it is important to know and talk about your past and where it has led you. Then I encourage you to let it go and start today by making the best decisions possible.

The beauty of life is that no matter what you have done or where you are, you have the ability to wipe your slate clean and start over right now, right here, today! Focus on your present decisions and look forward to your future.

This particular key to success is so extremely important. I have mentioned before that we cannot turn back time. Our lives are not a VCR, and we can't press rewind. Once we have made a decision, wise or unwise, we will have to deal with the consequences of that decision. When I think about this, I think about the night of my accident and all of the decisions I made or did not make. Those decisions changed my life, and created the person I am today. I would not trade who I am today mentally, emotionally, and spiritually, but I would absolutely love to press rewind and make different decisions to get my physical abilities back. Because we can't change the past, I want you to grasp the unbelievable importance of our every decision.

There are no guarantees in life. We need to keep in mind that every single day we wake up and take a breath is a blessing that has been given to us to enjoy and use to our full potential. There is no single day that is promised to us, even if we were to make all of the right decisions.

Key #3—Realize your consequences.

If we would take time to sit and think about all of the possible consequences that could occur with the decisions that we make, I guarantee our lives would be a lot easier. I think about when we were children and how we learned from our consequences. If our parents told us not to do something and we did it, we would get punished. Typically our parents had already told us what the punishment was going to be.

And then there was the conditional way that we learned from consequences. Our parents would say to us, "Don't touch the stove or coffee pot. They will burn your hand." So what did most of us do? We went ahead touched the stove or coffee pot and burned our little hands. "Ouch," we would yell, and then we wouldn't do it anymore. It is funny how the little things that we did as little children carry on throughout our lives. As we continue to grow older, those little decisions turn into big decisions, which then lead to even bigger consequences.

One day on my way back home, I noticed a friend of mine standing out on the sidewalk with a golf club in his hand and a golf ball teed up on the ground. He was facing directly toward the University, which was only about 200 feet away. I remember thinking to myself, *He is not really going to hit a golf ball at the University.*

I then noticed that behind him standing on the porch of a house were a group of guys yelling and screaming for him to do it. As he approached the ball to hit it, I interrupted his swing with a barrage of questions. I wanted him to think about all the possible consequences that could take place before he decided to hit the ball. The funniest part about the whole situation is that I knew that this guy didn't even play golf.

I asked him, "What are you planning to do with that golf club?"

To which he replied, "I'm going to hit this golf ball over the school."

I said, "I know you and you don't even play golf, but let's say you did get lucky and you did hit it over the building. Suppose the ball landed on someone's head. Perhaps the president of the school is walking by and the ball hits him in the head possibly hurting him really badly or even killing him. How would you feel, and what do you think would happen to you?" He stared at me, looking like there were all *kinds* of wheels turning in his head.

I then asked him, "What if you didn't hit the ball over the building? What if you miss hit the ball? When you look around you, what do you see?"

He replied, "Well, there are cars."

I nodded, adding "with windows that could be broken. What else?"

He appeared to be thinking more rationally. He listed more things, "There are houses with windows, and people walking by whom I could possibly injure or even kill!"

"What do you think would happen to you then? I asked.

"Well, I could be suspended from school, fined or even put in prison," he replied and you could see the wheels turning.

"How much money do you have? I asked.

"None," he said.

As I nodded my head yes, he laid the golf club down and said, "you are right man, this totally isn't worth it!"

As he turned around and walked back toward the house, I heard the guys yelling at him with disappointment, but at that point, he had made up his mind and made a good decision. And because of his good decision he wasn't going to be paying for any mistakes on that given day. This is a great example of evaluating the situation and realizing all the consequences before making a decision. I'll say it again because I believe it is important to repeat: please consider the worst possible consequences before you make your decisions. Never make a decision hastily or because you are being pressured to do so. That is trouble waiting to happen.

Key #4—Learn to persevere.

We all know that life isn't perfect, and never will be. There will be certain times in our lives where the ducks just don't line up in a perfect row. There will be blocks in our roads and bumps in our paths that will lead us to experience many ups and downs. This is a cold hard fact of life and that is all there is to it. We don't understand everything in life and never will. This is why we should be adamant about learning to persevere; or in other words, we should learn to be winners.

I believe we should program our minds to deal with

problems or situations that haven't even come our way yet. If you really sit and think about it, you only have two choices in life when dealing with any situation. You can choose to be positive or negative. It is really that simple. If you choose to be negative, all you are doing is making yourself miserable, and everyone else around you. Refusing to move forward will only make things progressively worse. If you choose to be positive, you can decide to accept the things you can't change, welcome new challenges, drive on motivating yourself and everyone else around you.

I choose to be positive, and I hope you will too. I know it is hard sometimes, but just remember that being positive is just as simple as choosing to actively and consciously think that the glass is half full. With a positive attitude there is no battle that you cannot win, and no situation that you cannot conquer! Remember this quote by George Bernard Shaw, "The people who get on in this world are the people who look for circumstances they want, and if they can't find them, they make them!"

I wish I could tell you that if you follow these keys to success nothing negative will ever happen in your life, but I can't. But I can tell you that with a positive attitude, you can handle anything. The more you think about your decisions and their consequences, the better off you will be.

Some might say, "It just doesn't seem fair. Even if you are making all of the right decisions, something bad can still happen to you!"

We will never make all the right decisions, but that doesn't mean that we shouldn't still try. I also agree one hundred percent that it doesn't seem fair, but the fact of the matter is we can't control other people or the decisions that they make. Take my aunt for an example. She wasn't making any type of bad decision at the time of her death, but unfortunately, there was someone else in the world who was making bad decisions.

I have a philosophy that life is like playing Russian roulette. Russian roulette is when someone takes a revolver and places one bullet in the chamber, spins it around, cocks the revolver in the firing position, and points it to their head. People who play Russian roulette are taking the chance that they might kill themselves.

You might be thinking, "Wait a minute! I am not trying to take my own life."

Bear with me for a moment. When we are born, as scary as this sounds, we already have a bullet in our chamber. The reason we already have a bullet in our chamber is because this world we live in is full of danger and corruption and we are unable to make decisions for other people. Why in the world should we add any more bullets in our chamber with our own stupidity?

If you don't wear your seat belt while riding in a car, add another bullet to your chamber. If you use drugs or alcohol, add another. If you drive a car drunk, or ride with someone who is under the influence of alcohol or drugs, go ahead and add two or three bullets to your chamber, because you are putting yourself in a two-ton killing machine.

I hope you understand what I'm trying to say. If you continue on with your life without learning from others, if you make bad decisions and not realize the consequences, then you are continually putting bullets into your chamber. Eventually it will catch up with you, and it won't be pretty. You could end up paralyzed like me, if you're lucky. It could get even more ridiculous—you could end up hurting or killing someone innocent. Or, here's the kicker, you could end up in a coffin yourself, six feet under.

Chapter 37

Conclusion

What you have just read is not just a story, and it wasn't written to entertain you. It is reality—my reality. I call it "The Ultimate Learning Experience," but it has no end. I can't say to myself, *That's it. I'm finished* and have everything be okay again. I can't quit this journey, and I'm not sure that I would ever want to go back—especially if I had to be the person I was before my accident. I was making foolish, dangerous decisions. I was burning my candle at both ends.

In any event, I'm not sure where I would be today without my "ultimate learning experience." It changed my life, changed my mind, and put a mission upon my heart to save lives—maybe even your life. If you are reading this book today, you have the power to take this ultimate learning experience as your own, to learn from it, and to change your life for the better. Use whatever applies to your life and make the decisions that you need to make today.

I know that you all want to be successful, productive citizens of society. You can. Just make a decision right here and right now to stay focused on all of your dreams and aspirations, and turn away from temporary fun which brings nothing but negativity into our lives.

Each and every one of you reading this book right now has different talents, different abilities, and a different destiny. Some of you may be doctors, some lawyers, some pig farmers, some business leaders; some may even be the future President of the United States. One of you reading this book today could be the person who will discover the cure for paralysis, and that cure will give me back my physical life.

You have the power within yourselves to be winners. Deep within you live desire, determination, willpower, ambition, and perseverance! This is just the short list of the virtues each and every single one of us possesses. What we have to do is dig deep within ourselves, reach down to the depths of our inner beings, grab hold of these virtues, rip them out, and apply them to our everyday lives. Every single one of you has a life, and every single one of your lives matter! Make them count!

Epilogue

You may be interested to know more about some of the key people I mentioned in my book. So I decided to give you the rest of the story...

Emilee Baber received a job offer at Duke University Medical Center in the Neurosurgical Step-down Unit. She accepted and moved to Durham, NC. I like to tease her that I taught her everything she knows about "quads." She is working on her master's degree in nursing and hopes to teach nursing one day.

Robin Clark and I became friends during my stay at Health South Rehab. We talked on the phone and visited nearly every day since that first meeting and visit as often as we can. He is my Obi-Wan Kenobi, my mentor. Robin lives in Charlottesville, VA with his dog Festus and continues his work with newly injured patients. He is also involved in many activities and organizations for the benefit of the disabled. He honored me by being a groomsman in my wedding this past January.

Josh Chiprut graduated from Radford University and moved back to the Northern Virginia. He and I talk frequently about life, jobs and girls. Josh has become quite the ladies' man. Who would have thought? (Just kidding, Josh.) He also honored me by being a groomsman in my wedding.

My sister Tammy returned to Virginia Beach after that first semester. She met a very fine Navy man, Brian, and married in 2002. Last October, she had a handsome baby boy —my nephew Blake. She organized HR Club Mom for mothers of young children, many of whom are also Navy wives. She spends her time with her friends, their babies and Blake doing fun things while Brian is at sea.

My mother continued to work part time for a while, but eventually quit her job as a financial consultant. She co-founded Chris Skinner Make It Count Association, Inc. a non-profit organization dedicated in its mission to educate and encourage responsible decision-making among youth, with an emphasis on academic achievement, overcoming adversities, and avoidance of high-risk behaviors such as drug and alcohol use. Her life is dedicated to the mission of saving lives.

My fraternity brother, Stephen Bailey, left a good job in Atlanta, GA and moved to Radford, VA where he and his wife, Bethany live. He serves on my board of directors and works along side me to further our mission to save lives.

My brother Patrick left chiropractic school and came to live with me in Radford, VA. He works as my business manager, booking my speaking engagements. He organizes the trips, making all the necessary arrangements. He honored me by being the best man in my wedding. He shares the vision of our mission.

I continued a friendship with my physical therapist from Woodrow Wilson Rehab Center, Suzie Jefferis. We emailed and talked on the phone frequently. After a while, she began coming to Radford for visits. We went hiking on accessible trails, roller-skating at a local rink, visited with friends, went to movies, and rested outside by our special tree on campus that we call our "thinking tree." Our favorite activity became our times of Bible study. Through Suzie, I found the love that God intended for me. Suzie Jefferis became Suzanne Jefferis Skinner on January 10, 2004. She is my best friend, my soul mate and shares in my mission to reach out to the world. We now travel together speaking to any and all who will listen.

• •

Chris Skinner's Make It Count Association, Inc. was formed to raise funds and make educational programs readily available to all colleges, universities, and school systems in the United States.

Our program includes providing presentations such as Chris Skinner's "The Ultimate Learning Experience" in assembly programs, followed up with materials teaching time management, character development, and goal setting skills at the school level.

For information on how to make a donation, or for information on sponsoring Chris to speak to your community, please contact our office. Please help us to continue to provide quality programs to our youth about the dangers of drug and alcohol abuse. We welcome your support.

Life Matters...Make It Count!
P. O. Box 1558, Radford, VA 24143-1558
Office (540) 633-2204, Fax (540) 633-6520
A non-profit organization (52-2401630)

• •